ISSUES

TRUTH

WISDOM

CONVERSATIONS

LEADERSHIP

FOCUS

ATTITUDE

Wisdom Conversations: Simple Truths for Those Called to Lead God's People
by Dr. Alphonso Scott

Published by HigherLife Publishing and Marketing
400 Fontana Circle
Building 1, Suite 105
Oviedo, Florida 32765
(407) 563-4806
www.ahigherlife.com

ISBN paperback   978-1-939183-29-3

ISBN e-book   978-1-939183-30-9

Cover Design: Dave Whitlock

Printed in the United States of America

DR. ALPHONSO SCOTT

WISDOM
CONVERSATIONS

SIMPLE TRUTHS
FOR THOSE
CALLED TO LEAD
GOD'S
PEOPLE

It has been my privilege to work with some of God's choicest servants. It was a joy to see the accomplishments we have achieved and the pleasures we have known while serving the Lord together at Lively Stone Church and the Lively Stone Fellowship of Churches.

It has been some of the high lights of my ministry. I joyfully dedicate this work to these faithful friends:

My Mentor Bishop Phillip Lee Scott

Pastor Dwight Scott

Pastor Lee Scott

Dr. Douglas Petty

Ossie Mills

Table of Contents

Introduction

Leaders face many issues today. Leaders in the corporate business world and leaders in the church. Leaders at home and around the world. Leaders, battling personal problems and modern trends, are experiencing a new season of change.

Should we go with the mainstream and avoid topics that may offend some? Do we capture the ideas of someone with a successful church and try to copy it? Do we provide a feel good sensation to keep the people coming back? Do you really know what it means to be a church leader? It has taken me a lifetime of learning from the Lord to realize what it means to truly be a leader.

My name is Dr. Alphonso Scott. You may have heard of me or maybe not. Either way, I have been a church leader for over 50 years. Before that, I was a military man. God has brought me through a lot. He has taught me so much. He wants me to share some of my insights with you.

You see, my father was the Bishop of Lively Stone Church before I was. Its success came from him as God worked through his leadership. I am one to give credit where credit is due. It is not me, but it is God who has brought me to where I am today. Many people measure a church's success by the number of attendees, but that is not what success really is.

God has shown me what it means to truly lead and that I am to share those things with you. Things that you need to know as a leader; for example, how to be successful at recognizing potential leaders. He has given me mandates about how to handle the tough topics like dissolution of marriages, abortion and sexual orientation. With that variety of topics to address, I write this book to help you stand for what God has asked us all to stand for and to become the leaders He wants us to be.

My main goal is to enlighten and enrich those who have a calling of ministry in their hearts. I seek to be a source of help to others. What I do isn't just about me and it isn't just for me. Leaders must do what we do for the right reasons, and the right reason for my leadership is to enlighten and enrich those who will take my place in the future. They will one day be where I am now.

I want to be that source they need; that voice helping them know what most leaders my age wish we had known at an early age.

One of the best ways I believe I can make that happen is to be stable. Too many of today's leaders waver and wonder; they aren't stable. I'm retired military. God has kept me through many crises. I've been able to remain steady and stable because of Him.

My prayer is that the experiences I write about will help you as a ministry leader to reach your goals in ministry, to find some form of glue that will help you stick. This should be that glue you need. This can be an assurance of endurance.

I hope that what you see in this writing is what God wants you to see. My hope is that what God has taught me will help you too.

Dr. Alphonso Scott

Preface

I recently sat at a table listening to college students as they talked about the problems of the world. They discussed their wounds, their scars, their abuse, their disappointments. They fussed about politics and church and war. They – though texting and tweeting while talking – spoke of the need for leaders to hear their concerns and value their opinions.

I asked questions. They offered answers, feeling welcomed by an older leader who would respect them during a lunch time of confessions. The students knew I cared for them; I wasn't just being nice.

The young leaders are future world changers. They don't need an older generation to just tell them what to do; they need us to lead them. They are craving spiritual fathers. That's what I noticed at the table. That's what I notice as I work on a college campus and as I speak around the world.

In books like "Wisdom Conversations: Simple Truths for Those Called to Lead God's People" by Doctor Alphonso Scott, the students are able to hear from a leader who loves and respects them enough to offer that needed wisdom in a healthy conversation.

They long for that type of leader.

Yes, I know. Leadership is a hot topic. Google it. Search for a seminar or book on leadership. You'll find many. But leadership is so much more than a popular topic. Proper leadership – from a biblical perspective – comes as people mentor people. Not just on a stage. Not just carrying a title. It comes as Doctor Scott writes, throughout these pages, in "simple truths" and in wise "conversations".

Doctor Scott has learned from years of experience. He has learned from those who mentored him. He has learned by watching followers make poor decisions. He has learned – while carrying that deep burden of true pastoral care – to sit at a table beside future leaders and hear their hurts, welcome their ideas and encourage their pursuit of dreams. He has also learned to warn them of their desires to lead with impure motives.

In Wisdom Conversations, the Bishop honors us all by inviting us into this dialogue. He addresses the issue of a leader's attitude. He reveals how church leadership plays out in today's world, and how true leaders can fulfill the Great Commission. He warns leaders of the challenges facing them, and offers advice on what to do about those challenges. He doesn't avoid sensitive topics: Doctor Scott includes his thoughts about sexual orientation, marriage, abortion, and leaving church leadership positions.

Whether or not they realize it, on-fire youth today add to a train of faith centuries long.

William Carey, not yet 30, defied a complacent church and became the catalyst for the modern mission movement. Following were a host of young mission giants including Hudson Taylor, David Livingstone and Amy Carmichael. Livingstone and Taylor were both teenagers when they committed their lives to missionary service.

In 1944, Billy Graham, who had recently graduated from Wheaton College, and 26-year-old pastor Torrey Johnson formed Youth for Christ. A young seminary student named Bill Bright launched Campus Crusade for Christ seven years later. In 1956, 29-year-old Jim Elliot and four other young missionaries were martyred while attempting to plant the gospel among the Waodoni in Ecuador's jungle. Hundreds of young people across America volunteered to take their place. As the turbulent 1960s began, Loren Cunningham founded Youth With a Mission. In the late 1980s ORU students Ron and Katie Luce launched Teen Mania.

Thank God for the unbridled evangelistic passion of youth. As Christian leaders today we're privileged to mentor their zeal, directing youthful fire where it can be most productive. Let's help propel young world-changers through these simple actions:

• Affirm them. As mentors to young visionaries, we must never be guilty of preventing youthful dreams from launching. We can help guide where those dreams soar, but we should never strap down the wings of vision or creativity.

• Challenge them. Let's help young firebrands construct a global vision. Entrust them with some weighty assignments.

• Inspire them. They don't want us to sugarcoat the mission mandate or minimize the hostile challenges against the gospel. They simply need to know that we will join them in the trenches.

Too often cynical voices tell young people their hopes are pipe dreams and that "with maturity" they will settle into (and settle for) a mundane faith.

Our future leaders need to hear wise advice from a Christ-like leader, one who respects the younger generation enough to deliver a prophetic warning from a pastoral heart even while walking with them through struggles, doubts and fears. They need to hear from a true Pastor, whose heart hurts for those who work beside him and those who will follow him.

Think about these pages as Doctor Scott sitting at a table with college students. At the table, ministers of various ages, denominations and backgrounds arrive. Many books have been read by that audience, many conferences attended, many seminars taken, many classes studied. When they've all finished voicing their opinions about what works and doesn't work, they all become silent. In his humble, wise tone, Doctor Scott begins to speak from deep in his heart. The audience treasures the honor of learning from a servant leader. The older pastors wish they had heard his advice sooner. The younger generation begins to realize this is more than a chat about trends and methods – they are listening to words that will forever shape their destinies.

Wisdom Conversations invites you to the table. Don't miss the chance to learn from a leader who cares like Christ.

— Chris Maxwell,
Author and Director of Spiritual Life at Emmanuel College,
and David Shibley,
founder and international representative of Global Advance

Foreword

I was, and still am, excited, when I learned that Dr. Scott was writing a book to strengthen the men of God to walk in wisdom. It is time for the senior men in ministry who have successfully remained steadfast in the pastorate to speak. Ministry is a commitment, and it requires the wisdom and knowledge that comes from God. It is for this reason that Apostle James admonished the saints, "If any of you lack wisdom, let him ask of God that giveth to all men liberally, and upbraideth not; and it shall be given to him." James 1:5

It is a blessing that a man, such as Bishop Scott, takes time to impart wisdom to those who need direction during this 21st century. I pray that you not only read but apply the words in this book to your life!

— Bishop Liston Page, Sr.
Presiding Prelate of The Greater Highway Deliverance Ministries

*"A leader is one who knows
the way, goes the way,
and shows the way."*

— JOHN C. MAXWELL —

CHAPTER ONE

The Attitude of a Good Leader

Paul Bryant, the former football coach most people know as "Bear" Bryant, made a statement that applies to ministry leadership: "Don't worry about making friends. Don't worry about making enemies. Just worry about winning because if you win, your enemies can't hurt you. And if you lose, your friends can't stand you."

Leadership and winning in the church is much different than in football. His thoughts, though, are for all of us. Worrying about the opinions of others isn't healthy leadership. As leaders, we should care deeply but we shouldn't worry about who likes us or doesn't like us. Leadership in the church cannot become obsessed with friends or enemies. We need to focus on a better question: Is this person developing?

Unfortunately, many of our people in many of our churches are not developing. Years go by and nothing changes. There may be a momentary change, thrill or some excitement. God, however, longs to guide His people into new territory.

So, what can take the church into new territory? Is there a trick or a trend to move Christ's body forward?

This is what is needed: Leaders.

This is what you can be: A leader.

Remember, the church you lead is a great ministry. The Lord has placed you there. Even though the Lord places the church in your hands, He never lets go of it. The church is an extension of Himself and He entrusts us to show others who and what He is all about. We must be faithful to do just that.

A good shepherd or leader must go before the people. It is good for a good leader to have a good testimony so that we can relate as the Lord gives us words. Sometimes personal experience helps the church to understand the word.

We go through the tests of life just like everyone. Sometimes it is good to mention that we have been there, too. This really helps. This is why we should sometimes mention what we have been through and also to realize that those under us have gone through tests, too.

The Lord has allowed us to experience things, but we must make sure that we do not use that as a platform to appear as though we want the credit. We do not want to cause others to get a false premise of what this is all about. It is not a good thing to disallow anything that God said is to be allowed. If we are putting out a message and are getting the credit for what God has done, we are not putting the message out correctly.

The key to leading is keeping the attitude and heart of a shepherd. It includes keeping the love and loyalty of our sheep. Once we lose the love of our sheep, we no longer lead but begin to drive. That is not always healthy. One thing that we learn from the Lord is that he was a great teacher and leader. He was the Master. He didn't lose the love, but He sensed that He lost those who knew better and He drove them out. So this is one time it is okay to drive.

> # The key to leading is keeping the attitude and heart of a shepherd.

Sometimes the leader can lose the love and loyalty of the sheep. Sometimes the sheep can lose their sense of balance. This will cause the leader to drive. This needs to be pointed out. The leader may take the exception and say he is driving out the evil. Others may say that they are taking on the mind of God and hating sin. If that is the case, the right attitude for the leader to take on is: "I'm not going to let sin beat me; I am going to beat sin."

The work of the ministry is to be an extension of Jesus. When He was here on earth, He could only be in one place at a time. But Jesus said that He was going to place things in our hands because this matter of His mind is going to be propagated all over the world because He is going to involve people from all corners. Think of it as an extension. We need to be mindful that we do not lose that and give an extension of ourselves instead of an extension of the Lord. We need this proper mindset.

Don't be like the rooster who thought the sun rose just to hear him crow. Some in leadership may be thinking of themselves more than what they are and their minds are warped. They are more interested in proving themselves than proving the work that God has given them to do. It is very important that we have the mindset that God didn't put us here for us to just sound ourselves.

This can cause an identity crisis. The crisis of identity is not someone else's. It is your identity crisis. We have to understand who we are. We are people who were born of a biological mother and father, but we have been born again. It's not all about us, but it is through Christ. We are born of a higher power. All that we do is to be done for Him. All that we do is because of His calling, His empowerment, His assignment, His leadership.

We must remember that during our battles. Who is a person fighting when we are preaching out of the Bible? They aren't fighting us because if it wasn't for the Lord, we wouldn't be talking the way we talk. So we need to understand our own identity and keep ourselves in the right place. By viewing ourselves and our callings correctly, the leadership role takes on a new purpose.

Understanding our own identity can be like the difference between my wife and me. She knows how to save money. When I was in the military I didn't get paid a lot, but somehow she managed to save. If it weren't for her, I'd be broke. I am quite liberal. God knows who we are individually. I needed to begin to learn that about myself. My wife and I were willing to be a team and make this successful because we knew ourselves. Our identities become realities.

As leaders, we have to understand who we are and then we will not have an identity crisis. The only time I have an identity crisis is when I think more humanly than I should. Every once in a while, I have a bout with that. Don't you? I have to ask God to keep me with a pleasant attitude and He will help me to come out of it and portray Him. It is important for me to be true to myself. It is important to be true to yourself. And when you do, and when you portray Him because of who you are as His leader, you are actually portraying your true identity. Nothing fake. No pretending. We lead by knowing ourselves and viewing ourselves the way God views us.

> # Leaders have to understand who we are and then we will not have an identity crisis.

When we look in Scripture at the life of Paul the Apostle, we can see that he was a babbler. He liked to talk a lot, but that didn't cause him to lose who he was, because it was not who Paul really was. He was one who looked weak. He was one people mocked, but when they did that, they missed his true identity. It was not himself, but Christ who he portrayed. It is very important to deal with our identity crises. Our identity comes out when we go through tests. It is through those tests that we prove our love to God. Don't just see the tests only as tests. See them as moments we are learning our true selves. Our identities can stand up. We can, like Paul, let God's strength be on display even through our weaknesses.

If we are not in love, we will not get through the test. Let us find that love and identity through God.

A brother may come to us and say that we need to talk more

about certain things or do certain things that we do not do. He may say, "You need to talk more about what people want to hear you talk about." For me, I do not battle inwardly about this type of thing because I could just sit and let the person talk until their head came off. For others, however, this may cause an inward battle. Because of the position in which God has us, we need to remember that it is not us. This can become an identity crisis, but who are you going to let be your boss? Jesus Christ is our boss, so deal with identity crisis.

We have leaders who have a God given character. That character doesn't necessarily mean that everyone is going to like him, but he has to maintain it because it is God given. We must exhibit the character that shows and then the character that we have. We do not want to show the character that we think we have. We may think we are just dynamite—not the Word of God, but us; not the works of God, but us. We need to be mindful that we show the character that God gives and exercise this all the time. The character that must be displayed is not just ourselves, it is the character of our God.

We have to be careful that we don't let ourselves ooze out more than letting the character of God in us ooze out. There is a difference. The Apostle Paul shows us this in that what he went through he could have said it was him, but instead he said that he couldn't have done it without the Spirit. It was not him but the Spirit in him which gave him the character to be a leader.

It can be the same for us. God's Spirit is at work in us as His leaders; that is what gives us the attitudes of good shepherds. His spirit helps us lead God's flocks along the paths of righteousness, and beside still waters as we restore their souls (Psalm 23).

Once you start doing things, you could be the talk of folks. Envy, jealousy, bitterness, and resentment may try to come in from other people. Don't let that stop you! What God has given you is a God given trust and it will develop godly character.

Again, look at Saul who became Paul. I don't think it crossed his mind that God would change him to the extent that he would become one of the main authors of the New Testament. He certainly wasn't small minded, but he didn't think that until the Lord interrupted his life. He had built a reputation of being a persecutor of the church and then became—when God gave it to him—a persecutor of the devil. The Holy Spirit used Paul's persona; he was an aggressive person. He was a person of progress in whatever he was doing. God used the same inner strength and gave it a boost. He became much more powerful until most of what we read in the New Testament is through his efforts.

We must have and keep the vision that God is number one. If we do that, we are going to preach who He is in spite of where we are. In spite of what we are going through, we have our eyes on Him. *Looking unto Jesus, the author and finisher of our faith... (Hebrews 12:2, NKJ).* That's a lot. We are admonished, as godly leaders, to contend for that faith that was once delivered to the saints. We cannot let it go. We should not allow the people to persuade us to change the gospel by making excuses that it is the 21st Century. This is a danger to the church of the living God, the one who placed us here in His stead.

God is the one who made it clear that the time in which He governs is not built on chronological time. The time that He is telling us to preach is not predicated on 2013. The time which He is telling us

> # We must have and keep the vision that God is number one

to preach and lead is dealing with eternity (2 Peter 3:8 KJV). That puts an altogether different scope on the message of a person that is human, just like those to whom we preach to. Somehow the people look at us as being just a little beyond human, but it is up to us to put it in the right perspective. I do not mind people putting me on a higher level, but I just ask God to help me to live up to it.

A good leader knows that a pastor needs a pastor. Have confidence in your pastor. I pastored, by the help of God, in a very small rural place. The town had no more than 1,500 people in it. It seemed like no matter what happened, I couldn't get out of pastoring in the town. It wasn't because I didn't get offers from other places. One time, I had a former presiding bishop come to that little hamlet to offer me a church with 400 to 500 folks in upstate New York. I rubbed my hands trying to be very pious. I said, "Yes I will leave if the Lord says so."

As soon as the presiding bishop left Nortonville, he called my pastor. He said, "I made an offer to this fellow Scott and he said he would move."

My pastor said, "He's not ready. He is not available."

The presiding bishop called me and said, "Your pastor said you are not available."

I could have said, "What?" or "Why?" because the pastor was my daddy. But I didn't. I had confidence that he knew what was right for me.

Every pastor needs a pastor. All sheep need a shepherd. Let's never forget that.

A few years later, I was offered a church in Dayton, Ohio, and again the Lord said, "No." I was still in Nortonville, New York. I wasn't paying too much attention until the Lord began knocking at the portals of my door and the school I was going to, the University of Evansville. One of my colleagues didn't come to the service, but they came by where I was and wanted to know the history of the church. I told him that our attendance ranged from 100 to 125. What he began to say changed my thinking. He said he didn't know anyone who had nearly 10% of a town's population going to their congregation.

So the Lord began to speak to me about accomplishments. It didn't matter what my peers were thinking. God had to touch me. God knows where we are if He placed us there. Don't let the enemy get you caught up in discouragement. A good leader knows no discouragement. Leaders see the table even in the presence of enemies. Keep seeing it. Be a leader who views from the right perspective.

A good leader knows no discouragement.

One way to help with that is to be careful about calling this "my ministry." If we keep saying that it is "my ministry," then the discouragement becomes ours. If something goes wrong, they will blame the one who is in charge. Most people do not want to blame God, so they have to find someone to blame. We shouldn't take that discouragement on ourselves. That's a burden that Jesus said to put on Him. We have to remember that all these things are coming against a God-given leader. Don't put yourself in a place of discouragement. Sometimes we allow ourselves to be in a discouragement cycle. In that cycle we'll go through pure hell because everything will be our fault. Maybe we should have done something or not done something. Remember your identity and you will not become discouragement.

God placed us in our churches as an extension of Him. We find our identity in Him. By sharing what we have gone through with our congregations, we help them to identify with us and they do not feel alone. We can keep the love and loyalty of our sheep by keeping the right attitude as their shepherd. And we are a good leader when we do not allow discouragement to come into our hearts. Having a pastor over us is a good way to keep that right perspective and be the best leader we can be.

THE HEART OF A SERVANT LEADER

The practice of Jesus is the religion of "the towel." John 13:4, 5 says he took a towel and began to wash the disciples' feet. We who imitate Him must learn to have the heart of a servant.

Jesus valued servanthood over ability, talent or culture. James and John were ambitious. They wanted a special position, but Jesus taught that there are no favors arbitrarily passed out in His kingdom. There are no Chief Seats. Greatness comes in heaven's view through service (Mark 10:34, 35).

When we become Godly servants, our hearts are humbled and our spirit broken. We move out of the number one spot and give that spot to Jesus. It is the same spirit that moves us on into service. God gives grace to the humble (James 4:6).

REAL SERVANTHOOD IS DEVELOPED

1. By the Spirit of humility, the way up is down.

Human pride is crucified. Godly servants are not to think too highly of themselves, but rather to think soberly of self. Jesus spent much of his time equipping his disciples, and that began by teaching them how to view themselves. The true servant leader does not promote self, but promotes, exalts and glorifies the name of Christ (Colossians 3:17). Every work, every program and every deed is to exalt the name of Jesus.

2. By the attitude of submission.

When the will of the servant and the will of the Master clash, the Master must win. That is how we grow although such growth is painful. Submissiveness means carrying out a duty even when we may feel reluctant. Following Jesus is not always easy: it may require doing some things we do not want to do. But in time, our duty becomes our desire! That is the essence of growth.

3. By the grit of faithfulness.

A good servant may not be outstanding, but they are faithful. Jesus said, "Well done, good and faithful servant" (Matthew 25:21). A faithful servant is dependable and perseveres. They endure to the end. Our prayer is: help me, Father, to have a servant heart. May my gratitude for salvation motivate me to serve, to spend and be spent. In Jesus' name, amen.

QUESTIONS TO CONSIDER

- How would you describe the attitude of a good leader?

- How can leaders obtain and maintain a true vision from God?

- What are the dangers of referring to a ministry as "my ministry?"

- What are your thoughts about the following comments? Every pastor needs a pastor. All sheep need a shepherd; let's never forget that.

ISSUES

WISDOM

TRUTH

*"A genuine leader is not
a searcher for consensus
but a molder of consensus."*

— DR. MARTIN LUTHER KING JR. —

LEADERSH

FOCUS

ATTITUDE

CHAPTER TWO

Leaders in the Church

Being a leader for God is a very serious thing. And I know that we, as God's people, need to be very careful about who we follow and how we lead. The Lord has to be in the center of it all. If there are folk... even kinfolk that are causing divisions, watch out.

I believe that God has something for you, but if you are not careful, envy, pride, fear, and deception can hinder you.

God has called you to a place to make a difference. Pastoring or leading others is a position that has its challenges and there are many things to be mindful of when leading God's people.

God placed you to be a leader of people and people are as varied as there are people. Each leader does not have the same pattern. God placed you where you are to meet the pattern in your church. You may work with the homeless or alcoholics. Everybody will come to you with a problem. Someone may come to church using drugs and you make a big deal about it. That's good because you're going to get them saved. We need to be careful that we do not put anyone on a pedestal. They could use that situation to elevate themselves instead of growing spiritually and elevating Christ. Other people come with other problems and a big deal is not made over them. All of it is unrighteousness. That is where the Lord showed me that we cannot be a respecter of persons.

> ## God placed you to be a leader of people and people are as varied as there are people.

There's a saying that if a Thoroughbred isn't racing, it won't do any good. The person you didn't make a fuss over could end up being the one to pull you out of the stall, and if the Thoroughbred could race, they would pull others in. It is important to let each person know the error of their ways. In this way the church will not continue to become more and more secular.

We need to remember that, whatever the Lord saved us from, we are not the only one. The person who was using drugs is not the only person to stop using drugs. The person set free from anger issues is not the only person God has helped in that way. The person struggling with unforgiveness and bitterness isn't alone. The person who no longer lies and deceives isn't alone. We need to make sure that we do not think of their situation and make more allowances for them because it could hurt someone else who is sitting in the congregation needing help in the same area.

Someone told me this story about a well-known person who came into the congregation one day and the congregation always held him on a pedestal instead of realizing that the Lord has saved other people. In this situation, it is not that we should disallow the person to come, but we need to be careful as to how we do such a thing. Remember, for God so loved the whole world ... so we have to take into consideration that they represent the hope.

One thing to keep in mind is that you are a reflection of God. You are an image bearer. As the leader, you get to call the shots either for good or for bad. Our conversation really plays a huge part. Tolerance has become a problem in the church. It is our job to preach that all sin is unrighteousness. A little lie is as bad as a big lie. It is all unrighteousness.

Our standing is that we have to learn, we have to study. If we want to advance, we have to be adherent to what the scripture says to show ourselves approved—a workman that need not be ashamed but rightly dividing the word of truth (2 Timothy 2:15). That's what Paul told Timothy and it is so true when it comes down to us. We need to keep that as a crucial part of our thinking.

A few years ago when I was pastoring at our sister church in Kentucky, I would have a Bible class every day. Teaching these classes was like a real awakening to me. The same is true with what have you have been assigned to do. I said, "Lord, I hear you." I had gotten lazy and I was thinking if I teach two or three classes a week and minister, I was doing too much. God did not give this to us as a part time job. This is full time; to labor with people takes our full time. You can let other things take your time but rest assured, some things that were important didn't go. It's because the people we are serving are living out there. No, as we said about this gentleman who was homeless, he doesn't have a bunk in the sanctuary. He still has to go out there. We need to study to show ourselves approved so we can help those who are living outside the sanctuary walls. Not one of them will have a bunk in the sanctuary where we pastor. We must not allow ourselves to forget that.

Some leaders today want to deliver what they want to deliver. We are in a dilemma. I'm stressing this. Much of it is because of ministry. We've all probably heard people tell us, "I don't want to hear that. Some of what you said, it made me sick. I don't want to have anything to do with it. Whether Pentecostal or whatever, you're too strict. You stop this stuff." Well, it doesn't hurt to be stubborn to say and do the right thing. That is what we are called by God to do. That is how we truly lead the church instead of letting the emotions and opinions of others lead us. It is singleness of purpose.

> **Singleness of purpose is being right there because we know that's right regardless of how we are being treated.**

Singleness of purpose is being right there because we know that's right regardless of how we are being treated. It's where we should be, even though they don't want us to be. It is dealing with biblical theology that we must know we're stuck in the right place, even though they try to pull us away from that. Paul used phrases like "the tradition of men" (Colossians

2:8). This is where we are. We have among us, and even they didn't go to school for this, those who have learned to deal with our emotions. I had a person come to us not too long ago and he tried to impress upon us what the Lord did for him while he was in prison. Here again, you are dealing with people's emotions with the Lord. We can get caught up as though the Lord only specializes in certain things. As we're preaching, as leaders, we have to preach all unrighteousness.

We have to look at all unrighteousness as sin. What this particular brother tried to impress upon us was that the Lord had put him in a special position because he had been in jail. Then too, he was trying to sell a product. If I sell myself, this product would sell. This is part of the visible ministry now. If I can get myself where I'm sellable, everything I put out would sell. Churches now are in the marketing business and I'm not buying that. That 12-year-old boy said, "I must be about my Father's business" (Luke 2:49, NKJ). Business is business and we have to sell our business. When we sell it in a way it lessens where people are heading, however, it's a downward spiral. If we are going to sell it, it should be in the heading that we are citizens of heaven. Follow us as we follow Christ. No matter what people say and what people do we need to follow the Bible.

Along this topic of emotions, sometimes our most energetic and explosive preachers can start out with a message and end up in a shout. In the message, the people can hear it. In the shout, the people no longer hear it because it is all in the movement. The message gets lost because the people are too engrossed in the movement. Be careful to bring down the level from a shout. We need to try not to get so caught up in the emotion that we lose the message our people need to hear.

The shout often happens with those who know how to preach the drama in and to preach the drama out. What I mean is that there are those who know how to give certain types of messages. There are expository messages. There are topical messages. There are illustrative messages, and some people are in the top of their form in giving these types of messages. They know how to deal with the drama and give it out. There are some preachers whose sermons are really stories. They wear the story out from the beginning to the end and put little details in the story to magnify the emotion of the people. I've been around long enough and I've seen it all. If I am going to help somebody, I have to speak the way it is. Are all these ways of ministry wrong? No. What makes it wrong is where you cause the people to head. If it's still heavenward, it is not wrong.

People think I am crazy because I say I'm going to preach the hell out of you. I say this because the people listening to messages are still raising all kinds of hell. It is our job to get as many people as we can to escape it. This job is not in the hands of those who are in the world. It's not really altogether in the hands of laity. It's in the hands of those who have been called and do ministry. Those are the hands of the leader. We are to be learners and true disciples. While we are being sent, we can give out the truth of the gospel.

> We have to come up now with ways and means of how we can help things to be better among us.

Paul had a purpose in how he talked to the young man (Timothy) about success. He said you are not going to be successful if you are not going to study to be successful. We have to study to show ourselves approved or a success in the gospel (2 Timothy 2:15). Ministry is so important. We have to come up now with ways and means of how we can help things to be better among us. I can't stress it enough and it makes some of us feel uncomfortable.

I define success in ministry as following biblical theology. How does that apply here? Success in ministry can be found in the Word where we are told that obedience is better than sacrifice. Successful in Christ is not successful in man's vein. People may think I am where I am because of myself. It's because I had a man, P.L. Scott, before me here that has done a successful work. I don't mind giving credit where credit is due, but I do not want that to take away from what I must do. We need to do things the way the Bible says. That's important. People want us to leave the basic principles of what we've been taught and grab hold of what is being done today. That is a sign of success. In the eyes of people, they are right.

Sometimes we can feel as though we're on target and the enemy will make us feel we need to see it differently. I thought I was doing right in a paper I handed in during college. My current grade was a D. What that problem did to me and told me, "You don't talk to Me like you talk to the people in your congregation. You speak to Me. If you want a grade from my class, you got to stimulate Me." It was not a problem with me. I'm going to tell you all the truth because I wanted a passing grade. But what the Lord helped me to do is get in the Bible.

There is no private interpretation, but there is a correct interpretation. The Lord will give it to us because if anybody knows the desires of our heart, God does. As leaders, we have to understand that if we are earnest, God will give us the desires of our heart (Psalm 37:4). He told me if I got that paper and read the Word, He would change my grade. So I went home and began to work on that paper and I put down something different. I did not change the Word of God. But I put the right word in the right place and when I gave that paper back to the teacher, he changed that D to a B+.

God knows if it's going to be done, we have to get answers from Him. As leaders, we cannot be man pleasers. We're going to have to do it the way He said to do it. That is what really matters. That is the grade that counts. That is what can take us from a D to a B+ in leadership.

One of the church's primary roles is to create an environment for men and women to foster authentic discipleship. God is calling for a ministry now that will cultivate that type of true, genuine discipleship. Everybody who says they are disciples are not all speaking the truth. They may want to be disciples but don't fully understand what that means. As a matter of fact, the disciples whom God chose became apostles. They became those He anointed. Many are called but few are chosen.

There are those who say we need to be more conformed to one another. We can do this only by becoming more conformed together biblically. I don't feel that any particular group, if they really believe what they believe, is to dilute. I feel that every group should believe what they believe so that we can bring everybody together to believe the same. This is where the strength is. Man will try to tell us the strength of a certain religious order by the numbers of attendees they have. No, I'm finding out in one group that I have become affiliated with and I'm seeing people from all different kinds of persuasions, when the anointing of God comes to that meeting, I hear people speaking in tongues and rejoicing in God. It lets me know that the Holy Spirit is saying, "No matter their particular vein,

I'm gathering a people."

We do not want to hurt anyone's feelings. But the Master Teacher tells us that there will come a time when we will hurt someone's feelings, especially when we step into their domain. Where then are we to go? Many denominations are finding great difficulty in holding on to a true biblical line because of feelings. Many of us are associated with a particular organization that is having a lot of problems because of issues. How are we to deal with them? Are we to deal with everybody being able to come in, hug us and say how well pleased they are with us, but really some of them speak evil about us to others? Just remember, if you really want to lead, you cannot go just by feelings. Let us not try to justify where we feel God has us when really it is only our own feelings.

I have a responsibility of saying what's right.

While on the subject of the way we feel, some preachers preach hell, fire, and damnation, but do not feel that they are going there. Some of these are leaders people have seen and heard from the pulpit all the time, yet we read about the bad examples of their living. Yet, people still run to hear their preaching. There is a certain way of life that I feel is bad and they should be glad I'm not God. These leaders are living such a life and are dictating to people they can live anyway they like and still be okay. They are giving the church a lot of problems. I've had people come to me and say, "Such and such a person is doing this, and such and such a person doing that." I'm not worried about such and such a person. I have a responsibility of saying what's right. It's okay to tell people what they should not do. Thou shall not steal. Thou shalt not kill. I can get by with that. Thou shall not commit adultery. I can get by with that. It's not being dictatorial. Thou shall not bear false witness. I can get by with that biblically. A man shall not lie down with a man or a woman with a woman. I can get by with that because it is not me being dictatorial. I am citing according to biblical passages. I think this is where God want us to be more accurate in our demeanor, not being dictatorial in using our leadership role as a whip. I believe forgiveness should be taught more in a way that would help instead of being offensive. There is nothing wrong with doing the job that God has given us to do. What's very important is to do it. God has given us a mandate.

Knowing about what God has said isn't enough. Telling others we believe what God has said isn't enough. We must live it out. Leading the church involves obeying what God has instructed us to do. Though we're all different and unique, we must learn from what God is teaching us.

Everyone does not have the same thing before them on which God will "grade" them. There are rewards even to the heights of royalty. There are five crowns mentioned that we receive. We ought not to mind receiving all five of them, if that is the will of God, but we don't want to get to heaven and receive none. We all have to give an account of the deeds we've done. There are things that you and I have done before we got saved that are thrown in the sea of forgetfulness, but we have to be careful of things we do after we surrendered our lives to the Lord. For things that we did after we got saved and for which we did not receive forgiveness, we are still in trouble. Repentance and forgiveness don't leave us until the end. God always gives us room to ask for forgiveness and repentance. When He saved you, He saved you initially to be saved. That's what we should teach. While we are being saved, we are being saved to be saved. We go through it until the ultimate. The ultimate is when God calls us. Isn't that wonderful?

I don't believe that God, in His infinite mercy and kindness, would put something on us that we cannot bear and expect us to do it. We do not always want to do it. We don't want to go through the heaviness. We don't want to go through being ostracized or criticized. "I don't want to go around with Scott because Scott is always talking about being heaven bound. I want to talk about where we are so we can be free of it." We lose our true identity of heavenward because of what will help us in the now. Preachers, we are now in a dilemma. Regardless of where we are, we are seeing men and women of every major denomination caught up, and then there are the people to whom we are preaching. Now where do we feel that the majority of these people are going to settle when they see all of this? They hear one thing, but they see another. We need to figure out how to bring change.

Our leadership is not built on being average.

I do not want us to be average leaders. Our leadership is not built on being average. That is something I say here all the time. Average is for people outside of the pulpit. God doesn't do average things. He does those things which are super, above all that we can think or ask or imagine (Ephesians 3:20). He is above average. The ministry is not an average vocation. It is a worthy vocation. That is the reason why studying is so important when it comes to ministry. It is so we can show ourselves approved, and rightly divided. That's not average.

When it comes down to learning what God is teaching us, it's just a simple word. A simple word. We try to use a lot of adjectives and a lot of everything, but I want us to realize that it's just a simple word. I cannot build up anything besides Christ. It is Him and Him alone. And when we teach leaders, with the help of Christ, we have to put in their hearts and their minds to teach that and live that.

Jesus can talk about Himself so much because He is the ultimate. There is only one Lord, one faith, one baptism. There is only one God and that one God is El Shaddai. He is the Almighty. He is Elohim. There is no one above Him. There is no one in whom Isaiah constantly said, "Who can be put beside Him?" He is all by Himself. He can talk about Himself. As a matter of fact, He is the only one who can talk about Himself and back up everything He says. That's the reason why He is the ultimate bragger. We can talk about what we are going to do, and we end up being late, but in Him there is no fault. In Him there is no lateness. In Him there is no earliness. He is always on time. He is God. Since He is God, and beside Him there is no one else, talk about Him because we want everyone to know more about Him. Matter of fact, I'm going to help you to brag about Him. That's my job. We should want to talk about Him. Let's talk about Him so other people will say there is nobody like Him. He has the authority. All we can do is repeat what He says. If we repeat what He says, we will be right about Him.

I've been around holiness long enough to know there are those who strut around just to case the joint. The Bible says we have to be careful because we ourselves can be fooled because of these types of people. Paul told the church in Ephesus that we have to learn the wiles and methodology of the enemy (Ephesians 6:11). He's no dummy, so we cannot become indifferent to his wiles. Somewhere along the line, we have to realize the seriousness of the lost—those who are not aware of God and His love, those who have not accepted Christ, those who need to hear the gospel.

We need to have a vision for the lost. We need to see the need of that lost individual. Sometimes we are so busy that we do not see the needs. There are some things that hinder us from meeting their needs. Sometime we have leaders who are indifferent. They will not let themselves be bothered. Some churches are very vocal or loud. The people are very emotional. Somewhere down the line we have to calm people down. The enemy loves when we have people so high they will not look

Somewhere down the line we have to calm people down.

at where they are. We cannot allow ourselves to become indifferent. We have to say, "There is somebody here who needs the Lord." We have to try to guide it. Sometimes, in the midst of all the hype, somehow we need to calm people down and say, "Somebody here needs Christ." Never forget our vision for the lost. God loves them. God has a vision for them. God has plans for their future. We should see them as God sees them, and we should seek to find ways of bringing them to Him.

It is our duty to lead the church. How can we really perform duty if we aren't loyal? And how can we be loyal if we aren't in love with our duty. Loyalty and love have a large place in the performance of duty. There were a lot of places where I had to go in the military as my duty, but that didn't mean that I liked where I was. I went because of my loyalty to my duty, but I couldn't add the other area to that because I didn't love it. When it comes to what we are doing for God's Kingdom work, we have to love what we are doing. That will show the loyalty to our duty. God has called us to this duty and we are to perform our duty to the best of His ability in us to do it.

LEADING THE CHURCH

The outstanding characteristics of a Godly leader are competence, compassion, consistency. A contagious spirit of enthusiasm and an attitude of earnest cooperation with these three characteristics a masterful time of meditation for thought and mainspring for action.

1. **A Godly leader is competent**

   This competency is both secular and spiritual. Those in church leadership are to be leaders in every sense of the word and, in like manner, spirit filled. Devout believers in the Lord Jesus Christ have their own Lord and Savior, their Master. The leader is one of the ascended Savior's gifts to His church (Ephesians. 4:11), and for their effective leading they are gifted by that Spirit with words of wisdom and knowledge (I Corinthians 12:8).

2. **Mandates in the Great Commission**

   This Godly leader is compassionate. A leader is a shepherd leading their sheep and not a herder driving some goats. Their conduct is marked by sympathy for the struggling student and followers, by tenderness for those who are taught, by pity for the proud and impenitent. The leader has mastery of his subject matter, yet is ever mindful of the needs of his flock, whether spiritual, material, academic, physical or social.

3. **This Godly leader is consistent**

   There is a steadiness of leadership, conduct and abiding strength of character. They are exemplary in attitude and in action, with a good sense of stability and propriety and likewise of relevancy of the Christian gospel to every aspect of life.

4. This leader is contagious

Contagious, not in the negative sense of being pestilential, but rather in the positive qualities of: buoyancy, optimism, courage, and enthusiasm. To this leader, life is an adventure and he delights in leading adventuresome, souls beyond the well worn paths of book learning into all fields of achievement.

5. The Godly leader is cooperative

He is cooperative with his fellow laborers, with the administration, and, of course, with his students or subjects. There is concurrence in the basic aims and objectives of the community and a glad conformity to its principles and practices. There is hearty accord with its affirmation of faith and a genuine contribution to the academic and spiritual effectiveness of the church.

QUESTIONS TO CONSIDER:

- Do you truly believe God has called you to make a difference?

- What are some of the ways you can make a difference?

- How can you help others to be leaders who also made a difference?

- What does it mean that Jesus is "the ultimate?"

- Why is it important for church leaders to have a vision for the lost?

"Example is leadership."

— ALBERT SCHWEITZER —

CHAPTER THREE

Three Mandates in the Great Commission

We need to have reasons for doing whatever we are doing. As we lead, we should know why. Biblical goals should be the true goals of each leader. Nothing should sidetrack us. We must stay true to our God-given purpose. Let's think about why, and let's study these true goals to be sure we are stepping forward correctly as leaders.

The church belongs to Jesus Christ. He gives direction; we leaders do not. We bring our directions in line with what He says in order to get the true biblical mandates. It is very important that we remember that these are biblical mandates, not just opinions or preferences, not just trends or desires. These are mandates from God which help us focus on why we do what we do.

Mandates from God which helps us focus on why we do what we do.

God has always had a hand in dealing with His remnant, of dealing with His church. God has also had to deal with men and women of great minds because people will follow them. Even today, there are great minds that people are following, but they are not all biblical. If that is the case, we will not get actual direction for the church because someone is setting up their own direction and where they feel the church needs to be. As preachers, we should be able to see this because that is what can cause our churches to become messed up. This is why we need to ask the Lord to get *us* out of the way and give us *His* thoughts.

We can see His direction given to the church in what we like to call the Great Commission. The first thing God commands us to do is GO. To go is to evangelize. "Go" in layman's terms is an active word. You can't go and be sitting still. That's the reason why evangelism is important for the church. It means that you leave where you are and go someplace. The One who is in charge gives the direction. He knows where He's called you to go. He knows your gifts and talents. The problem we have in the church is people have gone but they weren't sent. Jesus Christ, though, says to GO. He will support you. He will empower you. He will furnish you with the provision as you go.

Jesus is the right Man. Jesus is it, and beside Him there is no one else. Quit trying to let your buddy tell you what to do. Biblically, it's a mandate.

We are to evangelize with as much power, fortitude and help as we can get from God. Our problem with this is that we look at the visible church today and we seem to lose our strength. The Bible says, *Be strong in the Lord and in the power of His might* (Ephesians 6:10, NKJ). This whole business belongs to Him. These mandates are given by Him. Anytime someone looks to us, they are looking in the wrong direction. We need to look to Jesus who is the author and finisher of our faith.

In Luke, we see that Jesus said His disciples would be endued with power from on high (Luke 24:49, NKJ). Jesus was going to be the one to clothe them in this virtue and power from on high. No one could do this except Him. Jesus was going to give them the authority to go and do what needed to be done. He is going to do the same for you, but He said they had to wait (Luke 24:49, NIV).

Just as the disciples had to wait, sometimes the person with the calling has to wait. Do not be afraid to tell someone that they need to wait. This time of waiting is to wait until the Lord dresses them in power to do the calling. We cannot go down to the department store and buy clothes that bring this power. We must wait for the Lord to endue us with the power to get the job done.

The power comes upon us so we can go. It doesn't come just to let us feel something good. We become empowered, like in Acts 2, so we can go. They received power to be sent out. We receive power to be sent out. Going is part of the mandate. Remember: this whole business belongs to Him.

But you will receive power when the Holy Spirit comes on you; and you will be my witnesses in Jerusalem, and in all Judea and Samaria, and to the ends of the earth (Acts 1:8, NIV).

You did not choose me, but I chose you and appointed you so that you might go and bear fruit—fruit that will last—and so that whatever you ask in my name the Father will give you (John 15:16, NIV).

How, then, can they call on the one they have not believed in? And how can they believe in the one of whom they have not heard? And how can they hear without someone preaching to them? And how can anyone preach unless they are sent? As it is written: "How beautiful are the feet of those who bring good news!" (Romans 10:14-15, NIV).

Being those who bring the good news requires us to go. Being those who lead others into bringing good news requires us to go. We can't just stay as we are and where we are. We must move forward into this adventure of leading others into the kingdom.

> **The next part of the Great Commission brings us to the second biblical mandate which is to teach.**

The next part of the Great Commission brings us to the second biblical mandate which is to TEACH. Jesus told the disciples to *teach them to observe all things that I have commanded you.* (Matthew 28:20, NKJ). In Luke 24:47, He emphasizes preach. So this is very important.

We need to teach what really is priority. No matter what else we may do, Christ needs to be first. *Only let your conduct be worthy of the gospel of Christ, so that whether I come and see you or am absent, I may hear of your affairs, that you stand fast in one spirit, with one mind striving together for the faith of the gospel...* (Philippians 1:27, NKJ). Our conversation should, as we walk, show where we are and who we are. We are citizens here, but we are to let people know that our citizenship is in heaven. (Philippians 3:20 NKJ) Our conversation, our actions, our conduct, the way we walk, the way we talk, the way we carry ourselves, all needs to be heavenward. People need to see that. This will show people our priority, which is Christ.

Then we are to teach what Jesus came to earth for. In Luke 24, we see the account of why Jesus died. Verse 47 says, *and that repentance and remission of sins should be preached in His name to all nations...*(NKJ). The reason we are to go and the thing we are to teach is that Jesus died so we could repent from our sins and be forgiven. The Message puts it this way, *a total life-change through the forgiveness of sins is proclaimed in His name to all nations.*

Teaching is crucial for leadership development. Without teaching, we will be without leaders. And if leaders teach incorrectly, we leave ourselves with leaders who are not following the way of Christ. Scripture states over and over again the importance of teaching.

All Scripture is God-breathed and is useful for teaching, rebuking, correcting and training in righteousness, so that the servant of God may be thoroughly equipped for every good work (2 Timothy 3:16-17, NIV).

Do not conform to the pattern of this world, but be transformed by the renewing of your mind. Then you will be able to test and approve what God's will is—his good, pleasing and perfect will (Romans 12:2, NIV).

Then Jesus came to them and said, "All authority in heaven and on earth has been given to me. Therefore go and make disciples of all nations, baptizing them in the name of the Father and of the Son and of the Holy Spirit, and teaching them to obey everything I have commanded you. And surely I am with you always, to the very end of the age" (Matthew 28:18-20, NIV).

But seek first his kingdom and his righteousness, and all these things will be given to you as well (Matthew 6:33, NIV).

You know that the household of Stephanas were the first converts in Achaia, and they have devoted themselves to the service of the Lord's people. I urge you, brothers and sisters, to submit to such people and to everyone who joins in the work and labors at it (1 Corinthians 16:15-16, NIV).

A word of warning: those who keep the biblical mandate are going to get the fiery darts hurled at them. "Kill them. Get them out of the way." That's what they did to Christ. It's because as long as that person, man or woman, is standing up for biblical mandates, they are getting in the way of my progress as a human being. As a matter of fact, I've had people in our fellowship who said, "I want to go to a church where I can be free." Now they're telling me something. They're saying they don't want to follow what is being taught here. They want to go where they can feel free to do what they want to do. If that is the case, where are the biblical mandates?

This shouldn't stop us from doing our part in the Great Commission. In Mark 16:15-16 Jesus said, *"Go into all the world and preach the gospel to every creature. He who believes and is baptized will* be saved..." (NKJ). Which brings us to the third biblical mandate, BAPTIZE. Once we have gone to the nations and taught them about Jesus and forgiveness of sins, we are to baptize those who believe. Baptism is an outward declaration of what Jesus has done for us.

Think of the act of baptism. The event proves again the importance of publically proclaiming beliefs. Leaders do that. They don't hold back. They receive the mandate and pursue the honor of baptism.

Imagine being there to see Jesus let John the Baptist place Him in the water. That is a wonderful testimony of obedience and submission.

Therefore, I urge you, brothers and sisters, in view of God's mercy, to offer your bodies as a living sacrifice, holy and pleasing to God— this is your true and proper worship (Romans 12:1, NIV).

Jesus answered, "Very truly I tell you, no one can enter the kingdom of God unless they are born of water and the Spirit..." (John 3:5, NIV).

Blessed are those who wash their robes, that they may have the right to the tree of life and may go through the gates into the city (Revelation 22:14, NIV).

Those who accepted his message were baptized, and about three thousand were added to their number that day (Acts 2:41, NIV).

Or don't you know that all of us who were baptized into Christ Jesus were baptized into his death? We were therefore buried with him through baptism into death in order that, just as Christ was raised from the dead through the glory of the Father, we too may live a new life. For if we have been united with him in a death like his, we will certainly also be united with him in a resurrection like his.

For we know that our old self was crucified with him so that the body ruled by sin might be done away with, that we should no longer be slaves to sin—because anyone who has died has been set free from sin (Romans 6:3-7, NIV).

Don't you love those words: set free from sin? That is what has happened. The victory is ours. It belongs to us. The water reminds us that we are washed clean.

We have talked about how to have the correct attitude as a shepherd. We have emphasized what it really means to lead a church. But how are those principles applied? What should flavor all that we do as leaders? Go and Teach and Baptize: those three words help us stay on course. Let's not just try to lead for the sake of leading. Let's not just pursue a trend. Let's not go after big numbers or popularity. Let's disciple and train Christ's followers to go, to teach, and to baptize.

Go and Teach and Baptize: those three words help us stay on course.

By remembering those words, we can stay on focus as leaders. Getting "off focus" can lead to confusion, conflict, and unnecessary work. Staying "on focus" let's us follow the direction of the One who leads the church: Jesus Christ. He leads us. As we follow His leading, we can focus on those key components of what we are truly called to do.

Those are the three most important biblical mandates we see in what we call *the Great Commission*: Go, Teach, Baptize. There are many other things the church would be right in doing, but these three should not be forgotten and should take precedence over all the rest. This is what Jesus commanded all of us to do.

KEEPING GOD'S PRIORITY OUR PRIORITY AS LEADERS

Another key characteristic of a Godly leader is following God's plan. Keeping His priority as the leader's priority means God is truly leading. Assessment, evaluation, and conclusions must all be based upon remaining in line with God's priority list. Man's lists go in other directions. God's list is the one leaders must follow.

1. Know the mandates personally

Think about that leader who is inside you. As leaders who are called to change the world we must begin right at our own hearts. Don't begin it all with a sermon or a lecture. Begin when looking in the mirror. You are that leader. You are the key to bringing change. But start inside. Know yourself. Pursue change in your own life before pushing for changes in others. Look at your strategic lists and ask yourself questions about how they fit in your own life.

2. Make the mandates known clearly

Think about the best way to explain your guidelines to those you lead. Remember again: you are a shepherd leading your sheep. Know their language. Know their expectations. Know your followers personally, not just professionally. Jesus spent time with His followers and got to know them well. Through those relationships you can clearly declare your mandates to your team. Some will listen and learn differently than others. By knowing them better, you can speak to them better. You can lead them better.

3. Refuse to wander from the mandates of God

Think about how to best stay true to God's calling. To waver from God's word is to enter dangerous territory. Yes, adjust how you speak the truth but never change the truth your leaders need to learn and live. Churches too often change for whatever feels good. Or whatever looks good. You must lead with an assurance that you are staying true to God's truth. Do not waver! Stay on course (1 Corinthians 15:58).

QUESTIONS TO CONSIDER

- Go, teach, and baptize are the three keys for kingdom leadership. Describe how you are seeking to reach each of those goals.

- What can you do to improve?

- In today's modern churches, which of those three points seem to be lacking?

- How can you train leaders to see that change?

"*A true and safe leader is likely to be one who has no desire to lead, but is forced into a position of leadership by the inward pressure of the Holy Spirit and the press of the external situation.*"

— A. W. TOZER —

CHAPTER FOUR

Challenges in Being A Leader

Let's start off with an encounter I had recently. This will show you a challenge I believe every leader faces at some time in their ministry.

When I pulled in for Bible class, I saw someone sitting down smoking. He wasn't even hiding it. So at the end of the class, I usually go into some sort of an anointing service and prayer. I asked God to let the Lord's presence come in that would invite that anointing. I know it was the Lord who called this individual to the front. I won't tell every preacher to do this because I know what can happen. I have to teach what's right, even though I know what might happen. But the Bible taught me long ago – you watch as well as you pray.

When the subject came up, I started talking to the person and said, "Did I see you smoking out there?"

He said, "Yes."

I said, "You shouldn't be doing that. I had been authorized not to smoke. The Lord told me not to smoke."

He said, "The Lord told me I could smoke."

I said, "No, He didn't."

He said, "Yes, He did. He told me I could smoke."

I said, "The Lord did not tell you that. The Lord did not tell you that you could smoke."

He said, "Yes, He did because I am not of this world and He speaks directly to me and tells me what I can do."

I said, "Now, whoever is telling you this is a liar. You did not hear that from God. God does not tell a lie and God did not tell you to smoke."

Well, I guess the membership at large started praying because they didn't know what was going to be the outcome. The Lord will let you know what is happening. So, I said, "We're going to pray."

I had known this person since he was a teenager. But now he was in his 50s. So there we were, everybody praying, and he started speaking in tongues. I didn't bother him yet. After we slowed down from our praying – I wasn't through praying - I said to him, "Sit down!"

I had two ministers sitting on each side of him. After I said what I said to him, he had the nerve to speak in tongues! Well, I'm going to tell you - there were not too many more people in the whole congregation than at that meeting. They knew what I was going to say. And even after all that, he was still trying to tell me that the Lord told him he could smoke.

I said, "The Lord did not tell you that, son. You are a spokesman of the adversary." I was seeing the demon in him that gave him the boldness to stand where he was. I wished that the Lord would have touched him and we would have seen him relieved of that demon. But he wasn't and he left our meeting still the same. Then I was just worried about how many people in the congregation were going to pity him and say, "The pastor really jumped on you!"

I'm just waiting to see what happens next. Somewhere down the line, they will turn it around and some people will really feel like they have the right to do whatever they are doing, even if it is contrary to scripture. They can come right into your congregation while you are ministering and do things and not feel bad about it at all. What should we do? We have to proclaim biblical doctrine and theology because the philosophy of man is being given to so many people.

> We have to proclaim biblical doctrine and theology because the philosophy of man is being given to so many people.

Another challenge is that sometimes we, as leaders, can be loyal as long as things are going the way we want them to go. When going through some pain, we can become disloyal. During those times, we're going through opposition. People are talking about us or doing things against us. People might be doing some of it, but people are not doing all of it.

Where else does that battle come from? A lot of it is the "id" - the self, the person. The id is more than who you think it is. The id is the true you. And sometimes it can come out quickly. Sometimes if we don't catch ourselves, the true you will say, "Who do you think you are talking to?" Sometimes as a leader, we train ourselves to be quiet. There are a few times that we shouldn't be quiet. We need to be humble, but not weak.

One of the things that we should not be quiet about is when people are trying to put the ministry in a weak position. I had a person tell me, since they couldn't have their way, "If it was our former pastor, he would let us do this." But that's not true.

I said, "If you were doing then what you are doing now, you were wrong then and you are wrong now. I'm not going to take it." Ministry must adhere to biblical standards.

A person in Christ does not backslide.

That brother was talking about moving backwards. We don't move back. When we talk about moving back, we are talking about people backsliding. A person in Christ does not backslide. God doesn't make room for backsliders. In the Exodus from Egypt, God helped them come across the Red Sea, then allowed the waters to re-gather in their place when it was all done. He destroyed the enemy who was following them. If they tried to go back, they wouldn't go back on dry ground. The weight of a transgressor is hard. There is a lot to these things when we begin to look at them and it is up to us as the leader to tell people, "Don't tell me that it's easy to backslide. No. There is something you've been holding on to for a long time and it's been taking you down instead of up."

Another challenge we face is that many want to please people more than please God. I have many pastors who are in my age group who feel as though people of today do not want to hear them speak the truth. I tell them, "Don't back off." Many lives are predicated on how you can testify of where the Lord has brought you. You've got to testify.

This is a battle because it's surprising to find out how many people think and believe, "You need to shut your mouth because we don't want to hear that. We don't want to hear about anything you did back in 1960." We cannot see how far God has brought us personally, if we don't go back to where we came from. Even those who were back there might not be able to perceive it or understand it. However, once they get Christ in their life, if the Lord should tarry ten years, those whom they will teach would not be able to see what they went through ten years previously. They are going to have to be profound about where God has brought them, and that's where we are now.

We also run into a problem when we talk about God's Laws. The people say, "You are taking most of your text from the Old Testament and the church is of the New Testament. So we don't have to follow all of those old ordinances."

The Bible doesn't change. If it was a law of God then, it is still a law of God now.

Then there is the question of, "How can church leaders maintain a balance between biblical theology and church ordinance?" The Bible is standard as it is written. Church ordinances may change because of the times we are living in. How can we bring a balance between something that does not change and something that is changing all the time? That which does not change, we preach; it's authentic. That which is made by man is subject to change from generation to generation. We find this is so true. There are things the visible church sees now that our parents and grandparents would have called taboo. There were teachings from all different denominations: Baptist, Methodists, Holiness, and so forth, but there were certain things that all of them would embrace – biblical standards like man was created to be a man and woman was created to be a woman.

Because we are leaders of a church, there is something we see everywhere and have to deal with. Many leaders are getting caught up in sin. This is being made known worldwide. One example is the minister in Florida who was outstanding as a leader among his constituency. He was presiding over an association, but got caught up and ended up in jail. It was not something that was hidden. It came out in the newspaper and all over the world through the internet. And there was another leader of a group that was almost treated like a god. He got caught up in molestation, impregnating young girls, and marrying them. He ended up in jail. That's happening all over the country.

There was one who began to portray himself as a grand leader. He was a profound leader and then he get caught up with some boys and messed up his ministry. It's plastered all over the media. I don't think I'm the only one who has seen this. We have to look at what is really happening among us. It is well known that a leader of one of the largest organizations was caught having affairs with children. This organization has paid thousands, if not millions, of dollars trying to get their preacher out of trouble.

It is not localized; it is all over. This is beginning to be the world's view of preachers. All of these leaders say they are men and women of the cloth. Yes, this type of thing is happening among women also. People are seeing it.

How can we address this? How are we to continue?

We are to keep our focus on Christ and pray for the strength to not get caught up with other's opinions that are not found in scriptures. People may come to us and say that if the preachers can do these things, then why can't they. Our answer can only be that these leaders got caught up in sin and we need to pray for the strength to stay the course.

Many denominations are finding great difficulty in holding onto a true biblical line because of feelings. How do we deal with them? Are we to allow everybody to come in and hug us and say how pleased they are with us? Truly, some of them are going to do that and then put us down on the other side. We have to understand where we will be. We know that there is some vast hurting, even in denominational persuasions. What God wants and what He loves is truth. Truth in love - always remember those words. All we can do is tell the truth in love. Sometimes we can tell the truth in love and love doesn't take it. I have had somebody say, "If you love me, you will tell me of your love a little differently than how you are telling me." This is where we are now. If you really love me, you would

> We are to keep our focus on Christ and pray for the strength to not get caught up with other's opinions that are not found in scriptures.

talk to me a little differently. In dealing with issues, we often hear people say, "I love God, but I don't want to have anything to do with church." You've heard that, haven't you? Have you ever felt that way yourself? Whether people accept it or not, we are responsible for a lot of things. If we are responsible, we take the hit. I've learned as a military man that I know how to avoid some of the hit. I get in the foxhole, and that foxhole is God. As a matter of fact, He is the only one that we can rely upon to help us.

The type of leaders we need are those who carry at the top of their list a faithfulness to the Bible. Our leaders must be true to the word of God. To believe it, to declare it, to know it, to lead with God's word as our guide – the Bible must be at the top of our list of what describes our leaders. Remember those words: a faithfulness to the Bible.

> **The type of leaders we need are those who carry at the top of their list a faithfulness to the Bible.**

Many of today's leaders are drifting away from that biblical foundation. Why are they? What is luring them away? The challenges facing them. One challenge is not being willing to face up to what the enemy is scheming to do. The enemy is out to get us. He wants to make us compromise and not stay true to God's word. We may be bombarded on every side. But we must receive help from our good Lord. He is with us. We can lead under His protections from the enemy, but we must not waver from the truth in order to please man.

I don't believe God, in His infinite mercy and kindness, would put something on us that we cannot bear it and do it (1 Corinthians 10:13). We may not always want to do it. We don't want to go through the heaviness. We don't want to go through being ostracized or criticized. If we look to Jesus and stay focused on Him, we will be able to come through these challenges and more.

GODLY LEADERSHIP CAN BRING CHANGE

We often hear that leaders are born. I use the term "born" because out of painful trials, people who have a strong urge to lead are then able to see where they can lead.

Luther wouldn't have put himself in a very dangerous position if he did not see the need. He went against Catholicism by attaching his theses on the door of the church. He saw the need for a change, and by what he did, he started the Reformation.

Wesley went against the norm for the Church of England in his day and encouraged people to have a personal relationship with Jesus. He saw the need for a change and did something about it.

Many of the leaders of what we call the Reformation saw in their time a need for a change because of the downward spiral where not only the world but the church was living in unholy ways. There was a visible need for a change.

Now, here we are. Do we sense there is a need, a visible need, for a change? If so, how can we do it? The question is how can we do this in this time?

When we are called to be leaders, we are placed in a position to make a difference. This is what Paul was doing with Timothy. He was mentoring him to be mindful that he could make a difference.

Paul did not spare Timothy of knowing about the perilous times they were in. He wanted him to be mindful of it.

Let's be leaders who are mindful of the times we are in. And this brings us back to following our three Biblical Mandates. Realize the tough times we are living. Choose to make a difference to those around us. And choose to lead many others as we follow the examples of dedicated leaders who have gone before us.

When we face the challenge of confronting others, we can be directed by God. When we face the challenge of refusing to waver in our beliefs or seek the approval of people, we can be directed by God. When we live and speak the truth in love, we can be directed by God. When we are willing to stand up and not compromise, we can be directed by God.

I want you to know that there is a reality of being on the Lord's side. The Lord is my shepherd and He's promised me that I shall not want. I know that not only will He give us what we want; He'll give you what you need. We can't let the cares of this world turn us from the one who gave it to us in the first place.

Yes, there are challenges facing today's leaders. But God is on our side. He has called us. He has empowered us. As we fight through those challenges and find victory, the world will be a better place.

WHO SAID IT WOULD BE EASY?

We are here today because of the leaders before us. They faced challenges. They did not pursue the easy road. They put their trust in God, not in the pleasure of each experience. God is the source of true peace and hope.

1. God is Our Guide

The road we take must be God's road. Church leaders often blame God for each of their decisions when sometimes they missed God's true plan. Let's not make those mistakes. Be guided by God not by fleshly wishes or hopes. See that His will is confirmed and then you can take those steps into the unknown (James 1:5).

2. God is our strength

God guides us into places where we must rely on His strength. You have gifts and talent. You have learned over the years. That is what leaders do – we keep seeking to improve and grow. Never fail to realize, however, that God is your true source of power. Through His strength, the world is changed. Through His power, words can be declared by us that will change our church and our culture. Don't hold back when you believe your strength is in God (Isaiah 40:28-31).

3. God is our comfort

God can give us peace in the middle of our leadership experience. Refuse to lead by paying all your attention on one accomplishment then the next. Choose to receive God's peace. Rest in the Lord and the strength of His mighty arms. Lead and take risks but stay at peace within (John 16:33).

QUESTIONS TO CONSIDER

- What "challenges" have your personally faced during your years of leading?

- How can upcoming leaders be better trained to deal with those challenges?

- Discuss these questions from this chapter – *Do we sense there is a need, a visible need, for a change? If so, how can we do it?*

ISSUES

TRUTH WISDOM

"*A man who wants to
lead the orchestra must
turn his back on the crowd.*"

— MAX LUCADO —

LEADERSH
FOCUS

ATTITUDE

CHAPTER FIVE

Are they Qualified to Lead?

Many come to me and say they are called to be a leader or a pastor. Do they really know what it means to be called? It is our job to discern this and to let them know what comes with the job. The Bible states that many are called, but few are chosen. Are they really chosen by God to lead?

There are those who will come and say they are called because they are seeking a position. They may seem to have the right qualifications, but only God knows the heart. It is very important to ask God to help you discern what their motivation is. What is luring them toward leadership? What is their true agenda? What has guided them in this direction? As we seek to gain their true motive, we need God to show us what spirit the person is coming in.

There are those who may have a very emotional posture in your church that seem genuine and Holy Spirit motivated. It is important that you ask God to show you if they are legitimately called by Him. If they have been drafted by God, He saw something in them that will cause them to lead. He knew the true reason to guide them toward your ministry. He knew what position they could play on your team. Remember, God looks beyond our faults and sees our needs - maybe not our immediate needs, but needs. We may not see this need, but God knows it's there. And God will place people with you who can help you, but you have to ask God for discernment.

> # It's very important for that person to understand that they didn't call themselves.

It's very important for that person to understand that they didn't call themselves. God called them. If they won't let God help them through you, then where are they going? This is part of being called. Once they realize that God called them, they will need to know the following:

1. Where they are going?

2. Why they are going?

3. How will they to get there?

Many know where they are going, but a leader who knows where he is going is different. If you are going to New York, you know where you are going, but how are you going to get there? It can be easy for someone to know where they are going, but do they know why they are going there?

Many take the time and effort to plan where they are going; they place value in planning where they are going. Leaders need to let that type of planning be a priority. Their goals should be known. They can't just wait around and see what might happen next. The desired destination has been determined. They know it. Their team knows it. Where they are going is that place God has set aside for them.

The real question is this: why are you going there? A leader needs to know why. He needs to know the true reason, the true motive, the true purpose. Back to that trip to New York: are you going because it's time for a vacation? Is this a business trip? There may have been a death in the family. These questions have a huge bearing on why you are going where you are going.

Leaders should be sure of the "why." If not, too many surprises can appear and hinder the reaching of that destination. If the "why" is clear, however, leaders can continue traveling toward their desired place and refused to be stopped on the way.

Next: how are you going to get there? Automobile, bus, train or fly, are all very different methods of reaching your destination. They affect time and cost. Remember that, in your own role as a leader. The method of transportation to your destiny is vital for your overall agenda. Leaders don't just wait and see what might show up first. The "how" is part of their plan.

When taking a trip, whether business or pleasure, you usually know where you are going, why you are going and how you are going to get there. Leading should be the same. You need to know where you are going with the Lord. You need to know why you are going there. And lastly, you need to know how you are going to get there.

God isn't looking for ordinary, He wants extraordinary. Being average is not where God wants anyone to be. Just being average is not part of his or her persona. One leader who wanted more than average decided to go 24 miles in the air—out in the stratosphere. He wanted to jump out of this plane and free fall so that he could break the sound barrier. It was not in his persona to be ordinary. He had to accomplish something extraordinary. In my opinion, I thought he had lost quite a few of his marbles, but not to him. He had decided this is what he wanted to do. Once he knew where he was going and why he was going, he had to figure out how he was going to do this. It took great preparation on his part. He had to study aerodynamics in order to know when to slow down and open his parachute. If he had not done this, he could have broken bones just opening his chute. He also had to have faith that his chute would open.

> **God isn't looking for ordinary, He wants extraordinary.**

It took a great deal of knowledge in the area of aerodynamics to know how this feat was going to happen, how he could fall as fast as he was falling and slow up at a certain time because going that fast, he couldn't open his chute. He would have snapped off some bones. Somehow, he studied it enough to know that after he got down so low, his speed would slow down to the point he could open his chute.

That brings me to a very important point. Once you know where God wants you to go, why He wants you to go there and how you are going to get there, it will take faith to follow through with God's plan. Faith can erase the impossibility. The young man had faith and he did the impossible.

Leaders with wise faith can lead like that. Their faith can erase the impossibilities they hold inside. What about you? If you have faith in God, it would help to erase the impossibility. Extraordinary!

God called, "Who shall I send?" and Isaiah answered, "Here I am, Lord. Send me" (Isaiah 6:8). He goes on to say that he is not saying to send him because he wants to avoid adversity, but rather he has faith that God will walk him through the adversity. True leaders will have faith that God will be there to lead and help them through adversity.

If someone is called, they need to realize that Jesus said to pick up your cross and follow Him. Denying one's self is part of the calling. Jesus also said that we cannot be His disciples if we are not willing to suffer. One way to know if someone is serious about their calling is to make sure they are aware of the possibility of suffering and then see if they still want to lead. If they do not think they have to go through adversity because they are a leader, they do not have the right mindset to train in leadership. This is very important to remember. If the person cannot accept the call the way it is, our job becomes much more tedious in trying to develop the leader.

Here is an important note of warning: I have had leaders come to me and say "thank you" for warning them that it wasn't going to be easy. Well, Jesus said, "...learn from Me... for My yoke is easy and My burden is light," (Matthew 11:29-30 YLT) Whose yoke? His! Whose burden? His! He tells us this because in many circumstances, if we had to take it, we would not last. Don't yoke up with a fool. You won't make it. Don't listen to people who are trying to give you practical application when they have not experienced anything themselves. Jesus said, "My yoke." If there is one thing we need to learn, it's how to put it all back in His hands. This is very important. "My yoke is easy." It is His yoke; it is His burden. We can't forget that. He is the leader who has experience.

We need to understand that this is the Lord's work. Not ours. God has placed you in this ministry, a ministry that is His, and He is allowing you to share in that ministry. It is not our ministry. You need to allow God to help you with that because you may not make it if you don't. We need to remember that God said, "My word will not return to Me empty. My yoke is easy. My burden is light. I will build My church." The Holy Spirit will let you know that you are in a position in which God is allowing you to be. If you truly believe that God is omniscient, then all will be right.

> **God had placed you in this ministry, a ministry that is His, and He is allowing you to share in that ministry.**

God knows all. It is easy to get in the way of God sometimes. I have to stop and say, "Lord, help me dismiss it." I must stay out of the way. When training leaders, you need to stay out of the way because sometimes we may sympathize too much. Let God do His will.

If you see someone who is willing to learn and has shown

themselves to be teachable, help that person to become what God wants them to become. In their training, it is important to let them know what they have done right. All of us have done wrong, but we need to lift up the potential leader. They need to feel a sense of accomplishment. Too many people put leaders and potential leaders down. If you don't follow the crowd in putting them down, they will want to hang with you so they can learn from you.

Young leaders need to aspire to something more. We need to pray that God shows us ways to help the young minister to keep a spirit of aspiring. We need to be mindful to walk with the leader through their adversity and whatever people may be putting on them. Having a sense of accomplishment will propel the young leader to continue to aspire to greater things. Nothing builds self esteem and self confidence like accomplishment. The more a person accomplishes, the more self assured they can feel. It is important to develop that qualified leader so they can share in the ministry.

Another area to qualify a leader is that of integrity and honesty. It is essential to remain honest because if you lose honesty, you lose integrity. How can a leader deal with issues that arise in the church without honesty and integrity? People seek advice from leaders. Leaders must deal with the people by being honest and, therefore, keeping integrity. The definition of integrity is "the quality of possessing and steadfastly adhering to high moral principles and professional standards." (Encarta) You can see how important it is for the leader to keep his integrity. The church needs leaders to hold on to integrity.

In the business world, there are those who make things happen and those who watch things happen. The same is true in the church. A leader is someone who is willing to make things happen. This is one thing that separates the wannabes from the real leaders. A real leader will make things happen.

Production qualifies and separates true leaders from those who merely occupy leadership positions. Someone may come to you and say that they are waiting for you to put them into the leadership position they desire, but I do not do that. I tell them to busy themselves with Sunday school. They need to make themselves busy long enough for me to see what type of production they are capable of and then I can put them on a schedule to become what God wants them to be. That separates a lot of people. Next thing you know, they are leaving our church. They say there is no opportunity for them at our church.

Leaders will come to conferences and I have to ask, "What have you done to go from fellowship papers to ordained preacher?" There are certain requirements to be met. It should not be taken lightly. I want to know, "What training have you allowed yourself to acquire, to obtain, to become?" As leaders, we are to train those who would become leaders. Sometimes you may train someone and they leave the church. This can be a result of the person having a false sense of where they think they are. The Bible clearly states, *"Don't think of yourself more highly than you ought"* (Romans 12:3 NIV).

> # It needs to be said again... it's not easy developing good, healthy leaders.

It needs to be said again... it's not easy developing good, healthy leaders. It might not happen quickly. It might not occur just as you want it to, but that is what God is calling you to do. That is what you really want to do, and that is exactly what you will do.

Now back to production. There is more to be said on the matter. Leadership production gives credibility to the leader. I'll say it again. Leadership production gives credibility to the leader. There are those two types of people in the business community: those who produce results, and those who give reasons why they didn't.

The credibility of the leader can be summed up in one word: example. If a person comes to you wanting to be a leader, ask them to give you examples of what they have done thus far. This will help you to know where to place them. Example: We are living witnesses.

As pastors and leaders in ministry, we are examples of what Christ has placed here for the betterment of those He has placed under us. Nothing builds self esteem and self confidence like accomplishments. If we want the people to see where we are, let them see some accomplishment.

I do not want us to be average leaders. Our leadership is not built on being average. Average is something for people outside of the pulpit. God doesn't do average things. He does those things which are super; above all we could ask or think. He is above average. The ministry is not an average vocation. It is a worthy vocation. That is why it is so important that we study to show ourselves approved and rightly divided. That's not average.

The next qualification of being a leader is to know no discouragement and present no alibi. There is a song we sing at church that says, "I find no fault in Him…" Wow! If I find no fault in Him, why am I going around talking about discouraging things? Why am I letting everything get on my nerves? There is no discouragement in the gospel I preach and there is no discouragement in the gospel you preach. So why present an alibi for it? We may take it on ourselves by saying that the failure is in us because it can't be in Him. Well, don't. Let God have it. It all belongs to Him. When we let go and put it in His hands, we are able to help others.

There are those who will listen to you and those who don't really care about what you say. It is our job to preach the Hell out of them all. This is because every child of God doesn't want to go to Hell, so some things have got to be eradicated. Every leader has got to ask God for the boldness to say, "I find no fault." Many try to say the fault is in the church. I say No! The church doesn't run people from the church. When someone leaves, it is not the fault of the church. If someone leaves the church, do not mention any names because you are not to take it as a discouragement for you. Also, do not provide an alibi. Whatever alibi they have, that is theirs.

> **A leader is someone who knows no discouragement and provides no alibi.**

We need to teach that this gospel is so precious and upright that we do not have to accept the faults people try to put on us. There's a song we used to sing that says, "Lord, if you see anything that shouldn't be, take it out." We no longer sing this song because sometimes God wants us to see some things that need to be straightened out. We need to straighten them out before God straightens them out. Certain things we need to understand because those who are under your ministry are looking for you to help them so they can help someone else. A leader is someone who knows no discouragement and provides no alibi.

I am sure you have heard people say that everybody has something wrong with them. We do not want to go along with that. All it does is provide an excuse. People want to hear of your humanness so you can talk about your being human and lessen your authority so that you can talk about what God can do. And God says, "Be ye holy for I am holy." 1 Peter 1:16. This means that I am not going to give excuses for all my human failures. I'm not going to give any alibis. People want us to preach about our disappointments, our discouragements, our off settings, but again, I find no fault in Him. If we talk about Jesus, there is no discouragement. In fact, there is constant encouragement. I can do all things through Him; I am more than a conqueror. If I speak of Him and I am His mouthpiece, I should be more like Him. Christ must be exemplified and seen and heard through you and me. We may cry just like everyone else, but we do not have to put that on God and the church. A leader will show that he wants to speak and be like Christ.

You know that Satan is a strategist. He is walking to and fro to see whom he can devour. He wants us to talk about things that put people at ease, but now is not the day to be at ease. Now is the time to be sober and vigilant. Preachers need to teach that, preach that, and live that as an example to the people. To give excuses is to avoid blame. It is to offer a defense against charges, evidence of absence. Or we could say to justify. We don't need to justify because we are already justified in Christ. So it is going to be up to us to teach and train leaders and ministers so they can teach this the way it should be taught. No discouragement; no alibis, be sober and vigilant.

A leader who can lead without being dictatorial is a person people will follow. Many today are saying, "Do what I say and not what I do." The way Jesus taught us is almost like a paradox because He is the only one who's allowed to be dictatorial, however, He did not do this. Jesus did talk about Himself a lot. He is the ultimate bragger because He can talk about Himself and back up everything He says. There is only one Lord, one faith, one baptism. There is only one God and He is El Shaddai, Elohim, the Almighty. There is no one above Him. Isaiah constantly said, "Who can be put beside Him." He is all by Himself, so He can talk about Himself. We should say, "Talk about Yourself, Lord, because I want to know You more." As a matter of fact, we need to brag about Him. That's our job, to talk about Him. We need to talk about Him so others will know that there is none beside Him. Jesus has all authority. All we can do is repeat what He says and if we do that, we will be right about Him.

How many times have we seen and heard great preachers from the pulpit and then read about their lives? They tell people how they should live their lives, but are not providing a good example. This makes the statement to people that they can live anyway they want to and it will be okay. I tell my people that I am not concerned with what so and so is doing because I have a responsibility to say what is right. We can preach the Thou Shall Not's because they are biblically accurate. This is not being dictatorial. I think this is where God wants us to be more accurate in our demeanor, not being dictatorial as if to use a whip. This isn't to say that forgiveness shouldn't be taught. Yes, we are to teach forgiveness. But I think it should be taught in a less offensive way. There is nothing wrong with doing the job God has given us to do. God has given us a mandate.

We often hear the importance of a leader needing to have a vision. A leader must have a vision. But the holiness of God should be that vision. A leader needs to remember that God is holy. This is important to keep the leader from putting himself on a pedestal and preaching his own holiness. The vision a leader needs to keep is that God is holy. I am holy some of the time, but I want and need to be holy all of the time. Something gets on my nerves and there goes the holiness.

The second part of the vision is having a true vision of one's self. When pushed too hard, the leader must remember who he is and who God says he is. The opinions of others should not determine a leader's view of self. That must come from God. We are made in His image. Don't forget that, no matter what else is going on around you.

> A leader needs to remember that God is holy.

Third, a leader needs a vision of the lost. We need to see the need of that lost individual. Sometimes we become so busy that things hinder us from meeting their need. Some may become indifferent and that will cause distractions to hinder us from helping the lost. Lively Stone is an emotional and loud church at times. This can be a hindrance. Leaders need to remember that the Father's business is serious business. Jesus was twelve years old and saying that he needed to be about His Father's business in the synagogue. When times get loud, we need to have the boldness to calm the congregation down and say, "Someone here needs Christ." Let's not forget that we are here to provide a way for the lost.

Remember, even as leaders care for God's holiness, our personal worth and value, and deep concern for the lost, leaders can't forget the wiles or methodology of the enemy. He is no dummy. We cannot become indifferent to his wiles. Somewhere along the line, we have to show the seriousness of reaching the lost.

That three-fold vision is a mainstay of a godly leader. We have to keep the vision of God and if we do that, then we are going to talk about Him. A true leader will say, "In spite of where I am and what I am going through, I have my vision in Him."

> ## A true leader will say, "In spite of where I am and what I am going through, I have my vision in Him."

The qualifications of a good potential leader are that they know who they are in Christ and that God called and chose them, not they themselves. They know where they are going, why they are going there and how they are going to get there. They need to show that they are teachable. A young leader needs to possess aspirations. Integrity and honesty need to be evident in what they do. Whatever position you put them in, they will produce much. The person needs to know no discouragement and present no alibis. A true leader will lead without being dictatorial. Finally, a leader needs to have the three-fold vision. When you see these qualities in a person, be willing to teach them and train them in the work of the ministry.

Ask God to help you see these qualities and know that they are truly called of Him.

Let the training begin…

GET TO KNOW THOSE YOU LEAD

This chapter is based on question, an important questions. Are those you are training really qualified to lead? What are their true motives? What has taken them to this place? Take time to get to know them. Find their true motives. This is not controlling them; it is instead protecting them from entering areas they aren't ready to enter. You often lead by turning on the red light and stopping some people from continuing their journey.

1. The who

Who is this person you are leading? Those seeking church leadership roles rush there too quickly. Take time to find out the real person you seek to lead. Give them time to be transparent and authentic. Know their spiritual gifts and personality traits. Also know the painful luggage they might be carrying. You are doing your ministry and them a favor by knowing WHO you are leading.

2. The what

What do they really want to do? Find out the answer to that crucial question. Do they want attention? Do they want a platform for fame because of deep insecurities? A leader who isn't seeking a role for the right reasons can damage their future teams and also damage their own healing. Your interaction with them can help determine WHAT they truly want to do.

3. The why

Why do they want to do that? True leaders seek to determine the deep motives of potential followers. Yes, maybe they want to do great things, but why? Internal motives can help leaders guide followers in the right path or the wrong path. Catch that early. Learn WHY they want to step forward into leadership.

4. The when

When is the best time for them to lead? This evaluation process is also preparation. You can see that some followers aren't ready, but you can also see what it will take to get them ready. It is a cleansing process. It is a time of training and equipping. See this from a positive perspective. Now is your chance to lead a future leader. Let God direct you to know WHEN they are ready to receive their next assignment.

5. The how

How can they best be equipped? Each person learns differently. They respond in their own unique ways. Find the best way to guide your followers then lead them toward their next great adventure. By finding HOW to lead them you've been led by the Spirit to prepare them to be world changes.

QUESTIONS TO CONSIDER

- What are your thoughts on this statement? *The credibility of the leader can be summed up in one word: example.*

- What examples in Scripture followed that strategy correctly? What biblical leaders failed in that area?

- What three-fold vision is a mainstay of a godly leader?

- How do you personally apply that vision in your role as a leader?

- How can you help others apply it?

"The fear of the Lord helps us recognize our accountability to God for the stewardship of leadership. It motivates us to seek the Lord's wisdom and understanding in difficult situations. And it challenges us to give our all to the Lord by serving those we lead with love and humility."

— PAUL CHAPPELL —

CHAPTER SIX

Dealing with the Sensitive Issues

It is necessary that we find a balance to these issues because it involves you and it involves me. We may not be going through one or two of them right now, but any of them could pop up at any time. We will have to deal with them. What is our take? What do we think about these particular issues? We can't scratch our eyeballs and look up. We want to come with a reasonable answer as the Holy Spirit prompts us and helps us to do so.

That is why we are not to put ourselves in a vacuum, in a place where we are not open to seasons. Throughout these pages, I have been honest. I admit to you that I don't open up too widely. We have to find out what allowances we have to deviate from biblical theology. Leaders, that's important. From all the text in the epistles and alluded to in the gospels, we are not our own. Not only have we been called, but we have been chosen. The biggest problem we have now with many is that they accepted the call, but as we watch them, we wonder if they are really chosen because biblical theology is our mainstay.

It is very important for us to understand there are cultural issues that are very divisive from biblical theology. There are many sensitive issues in the church and elsewhere, but we will bring light to three of the hardest ones to deal with.

If we leaders are going to take a stand with these issues, we need to make sure that how the church is expected to view the issue is clearly stated in the church article – or statement of beliefs. I often tell pastors, "If you are going to take a stand against certain things, you should make sure it's in your articles. Just don't come and say this is what I believe if it isn't in your articles." It is very important that churches and Christian organizations have articles of faith. If we say, "We are against homosexuality," it should be the belief of our group. We can't just come up with that because eventually what happens is people are coming forward and suing religious groups, accusing them of teaching and preaching hate instead of love.

The first topic to cover is sexual orientation. This subject could take an entire book to go over, but we will only look at a few areas of the subject.

SEXUAL ORIENTATION

When dealing with sexual orientation, we need to look at many aspects. The first is psychology – meaning the ability to locate oneself and one's environment with reference to time, place and people. It comes down to how people see themselves. We have seen men say, "I am a woman," and they begin to show a lot of femininity. We have seen a woman say, "I am a man," and show a lot of masculinity. There is a battle dealing with orientation. We see it in the streets. We see it in the workplace. We see it in the church.

What does the Bible say about the subject? Do we believe according to the Bible? The Bible says that God brought into existence male and female. He also let us know that each one of them had a particular function dealing with their orientation. Man is to have the seed that can produce life. The female is to receive the seed that can bring life into existence. Biblically, these are the two foundations of the human race. When faced with the question of our belief on sexual orientation and tolerance today, invite the person to show us that the same Author of the Bible said it is all right for that male not to use the organs that He intended for the male to use, to make the organs no longer functional. Or in the woman, the organs that He gave the woman to use are no longer functional. How can we bring some sense of balance to this? The Bible is a book to be believed and followed. Leaders must understand that it is very important to believe this. The argument, biblically and theologically, against a man no longer being a man and a woman no longer being a woman is a losing battle, as far as the Bible is concerned.

> **It comes down to how people see themselves.**

God has given the church certain things to hold on to, His ordinances. One of God's ordinances is that a man is a man, not a woman in a man's body. God's ordinances, or rules, always stay the same, even if the times try to change the way we see things. God set rules that we need to ask Him for the strength to carry out. Remember, we are to speak truth to the people.

Two places in Leviticus the Bible speaks straight about sexual orientation. In Leviticus 18:22, we see God's view on gender roles. "Do not have sexual relations with a man as one does with a woman; that is detestable" (NIV). Now, how can we understand that to mean anything different than what it says so plainly? Leviticus 20:13 is similar: "If a man lies with a male as he lies with a woman, both of them have committed an abomination. They shall surely be put to death. Their blood shall be upon them" (NKJ). Now, if this is wrong, it is a sin. Apostle Paul wrote, "The wages of sin is death" (Romans 6:23, NKJ). A person who violates these basic rules is violating God's ordinances, God's rules. This is not just a rule of manmade church.

There are traditions of man and there are ordinances of God. God set rules which we as leaders must ask for strength to carry out. All homosexuality, sodomy, lesbianism, beastiality – sexual encounter with animals – all of them are sexual perversion and are condemned in the Bible with penalty. These are things that are hard for many leaders to do because it is not popular, but the question is dealing with balance. That means something is going to have to be put on a scale instead of just what they want to believe. If it is just that on the scale, the scale is lopsided. Something else has to be put on that scale. That which is wrong is put on the scale with what God has to say. It is just a matter of how firmly we can give a logical definition of what is orientation of the sexes. If I am a man, I am a man. If a person is a woman, she's a woman. We are in the middle now of a mixed up society. We must ask God to help us.

Romans 1:18-32 gives us a parallel that we can look at. As a matter of fact, all the seven sins of verses 21-23 carry the penalty of death. As leaders, we have to know that God is not playing with this. A person who alters their orientation is going against God's order. Going against God's orientation – God's order of the sex which they are – is a sin. When approached by someone who does not believe the way the Bible states orientation, we can say, "Help me. Give me a theological base for you to say it is all right to be what you are not in actuality, not for what you want me to see because if a man has a penis, he is a man. A woman who has a uterus is a female. Whether they use those organs for what it was intended is a mind problem. It doesn't mean they don't have it; it's their mind telling them they are not going to use it." Now, that's not Greek. That's not Hebrew. That's just plain English. As the Bible has been translated into English, that is how it is written. IT IS VERY IMPORTANT THAT IT IS UNDERSTOOD THAT THE BIBLE IS FIRM. I CANNOT BRING A BALANCE THAT THE PERSON WHO BELIEVES HAS A CHANCE OF RECEIVING. If you don't believe, you won't receive and that is what's happening today. There are many people who do not believe the Bible. They say, "I would just rather do it the way I want it to be done."

How many times have we heard on the news about someone who

> **If you don't believe, you won't receive and that is what's happening today.**

is going to change their gender? It is really sad because a person can change what their physical body has, but they cannot change the mind of God on who they are and what gender they were meant to be. Cut away this and replace it with that. That is not what God did. This may go against what is happening among us now because that person has really decided to go a step farther. People say, "I want it to be completely the way I want it, if I have to get a surgeon. If I have to pay $20,000 to have that type of surgery, that's what I want and I am willing to pay for it. I don't want to be a man. I want to be a woman." There is no way, unless they come up with some other scientific thing, for a man, even though they cut away his sexual organs, to have a womb and have a baby. He cannot conceive and be with child. Nor can a woman produce sperm. God made man to be man and woman to be woman. Period. Is the church going to cave in or will the church stick to the biblical text?

What do we do if someone has had their sexual organs changed? If they come to us and want our help, the pastoral guidance is that they cannot go back. They're going to have to live with the decision they made. In the medical field, there are many criteria, many papers to be signed and the person has gone through much counseling before the operation can happen. They know some of the right and the wrong of the decision they make. Once they make it and do it, they have to live with it. That cannot be reversed. Does that mean God cannot forgive? That is not the question. That is not the unforgiveable sin, however, the

But only people who are forgiven know they are forgiven.

error of their ways must be made plain. A pastor can't give in to that because they have made the error. They are going to have to live with it. And when they give their life to Christ, they are going to have to go with it. That doesn't mean that they can't be forgiven, but only people who are forgiven know they are forgiven. Paul writes, "there is now no condemnation to those who are in Christ Jesus" (Romans 8:1, NIV). Once they are in Christ, all those things that they have done are forgiven. Sometimes the enemy will bring it to your remembrance. It is God who said, "Old things are passed away; behold, all things are become new" (2 Corinthians 5:17, NKJ). Our job, even in this case where a person has done something they cannot change back, is to let the Holy Spirit deal with that person so they won't feel condemnation. The Holy Spirit can do it, but it's a tall order. Then it's our job, especially when they come to us for counseling, to bring some balance.

Jesus said, "I have come that they may have life, and that they may have it more abundantly" (John 10:10, NKJ). It's up to the leaders to not shy away from issues that are upon our children. I get in trouble all the time because people feel like I should be more sensitive. I am sensitive, but I am sensitive to the Bible. I try to be sensitive of and care for the child of God who is in the church, but the person in the church must understand there is a rule that supersedes our sensitivities. We must be sensitive to God. In Acts 4:8-12, the boldness to take a stand came from the Holy Spirit. We should rather obey God than man (Acts 5:29).

In many congregations now, we are not seeing the traditional family. It is slowly dying out. In the visible church, we are seeing more single parents. How can we bring a sense of balance? There was a time on Sunday mornings when many of us had children in Sunday school. In many churches, Sunday school is dwindling. We have grownups coming to church, but no children. If something is not done, the church is going to become extinct. How can we bring balance to this? One thing is we are going to have to rehearse it more. Somebody mentioned to me the other day that parents and grandparent are going to have to become more forceful. Young people must understand the need because if they stop now, how much are they going to teach their children? Remember the command that was given in the old economy." Train up a child in the way he should go and when he is old he will not depart from it" (Proverbs 22:6, NKJ). It is our responsibility to teach because it is the only way it will be maintained. It is a sense of balance.

A parent recently told me that they didn't feel like forcing their child to go to church would be right because the child would just hate it. Their approach is not correct. Parents should force them to go as much as possible, but it is to the point now that you can't even force them. They are not going to listen. It's as bad as that. They'll say, "I don't want to go to church." They still eat your food, don't they? Yes, sometimes they become locusts and eat everything in the house. Yet they don't want to listen to how we can bring balance, even in the family structure. Paul told Timothy that if a father's teaching is nowhere in existence but you have a strong mother and grandmother who stick to the principle, you are still able to do what needs to be done. It means something today. The teaching of the Bible must be in the home while dealing with sexual orientation.

> It is our responsibility to teach because it is the only way it will be maintained. It is a sense of balance.

DISSOLVING MARRIAGES

Next is the issue of dissolving marriages. What is the biblical take on this? We can see that today a person can say, "If I don't want to stay married, well, so be it." It is easy to dissolve a marriage for any reason. Why should we give in to that concept when we should be trying to solve differences in marriages and provide the glue that will stick? Let's look into that.

There was a time that marriages could be eliminated primarily by the man for any reason at all. Today, if we are not careful, people will hang that on us, but we want to look at some things dealing with this. The numbers are out of proportion for marriages that are dissolving. It is not only because of men. We are finding out now it often is because of women. She says, "He is not as cool as he once was. He is not as sensitive as when we got married." Then the man feels like, "She is not as nice. She might have a nice figure, but she's mean." A lot of things come to bear. So now it is not just the man that is dissolving the marriage. It is both sides for many reasons.

Marriage has a lot of things coming against this union which God Himself instituted. This is biblical theology. Nowhere in my time of study have I found that God has done away with the original intent. If someone has found that in the Bible, we will look at it, but I do not see where God has changed His mind in dealing with marriages. The divorce rate is off the chart. It was common in the ancient world that men could divorce their wives, but the Lord Himself did not establish divorce. He brought justice to an existing problem at that time. God saw that things were going against what He had spoken. He will do something to bring us within the confines of what He has established.

In Deuteronomy 24, we see where Moses spoke of a certificate of divorce. This was initiated and prepared for dealing with the official document of that time used in dissolving a marriage. During that time, a man could have written it if he found any uncleanness in his wife. Scholars are still trying to find out what uncleanness he was talking about. No one knows exactly what the uncleanness – literally, the thing of nakedness – was supposed to mean. When we start talking about nakedness, we are talking about being uncovered. It was something that the husband found uncovered. Yet, the Lord does not give us so much that we give sufficient grounds for divorce.

In Jeremiah 3:1, we read "They say, 'If a man divorces his wife, and she goes from him and becomes another man's, may he return to her again?' Would not that land be greatly polluted? But you have played (in this sense) the harlot with many lovers; yet return to Me," says the Lord (NKJ). We find that not only are we dealing with the Bible, we are dealing with spiritual adultery or dissolving. We need to look at how God views divorce. God doesn't sanction separation. As a matter of fact, when it comes down to Him, it is to stick and be glued together. Stay. Believers today should really look at divorce and regard it as something that is not sanctioned by God. It is only sanctioned in the Bible when dealing with adultery or fornication. God is saying some other things in dealing with dissolution of marriage and we should look at it.

There are three things we will look at:

1) Right off the bat, marriage is a holy institution. When God created the world, He made male and female and established that they should be united in marriage. This is found in Genesis 1:27 and 2:24. The marital union should be characterized by singular faithfulness. God considers the marriage bond sacred. That's a big word – sacred. It even surpasses the bond between parents and children. The marriage is a bond between man and woman. It's

surprising some things people want left out of the wedding vows. Some people don't like the idea, "Til death do you part." They don't want that mentioned in the marriage vows. Our response, as God-given leaders, should be, "It's good to be in the marriage vows." A marriage can be dead. But if you think of it as sacred, you are going to try to keep it alive. God considers it as a sacred thing.

An example of a marriage being dead is not dealing with the man or the woman being gone; it is dealing with the fact that there is no love. That marriage is dead. There is nothing to keep the bond of that marriage. That's why when we say that the institution of marriage is sacred, love is of the essence. Love is of the essence. If there is no love, there's discontent, malcontent, ill-content, whatever you want to say—no content. That is the reason why in biblical understanding and for the child of God, if the person you are standing before is a child of God, then they are bound for certain ordinances of God to see that certain things stick.

> **If there is no love, there's discontent, malcontent, ill-content, whatever you want to say— no content.**

Love, because God is love, should be the mainstay of a marriage. It is God's institution. It is of God's origination. If God does not stay in it, there are problems.

Once a marriage is dissolved and if that marriage dissolves other than by biblical authorization, the Bible says that those persons should remain unmarried, but if the person remarries, the other person is free. This happens a lot. This divorce thing has gone haywire. Some people divorce; they don't care about how their partner feels. We try to bring some counsel to the grieving party while they are still in love with the person that doesn't care about them. All of these types of things are involved in dissolving marriages. In counseling, you are trying to preserve what sanity can be maintained or regained by a party because as long as you allow the negative thoughts, it is psychologically impairing. It can cause people to have bad health. Dissolving marriages is no easy thing. We have to ask God to help us. The main thing we need to understand is that dissolving marriages is not new. I have had people come to me and one party says they got tired of looking across the table and seeing how the other person chews. This is true. "I couldn't stand watching them chew. I gotta get out of this." And we would be surprised at what people come up with to dissolve a marriage. That is the reason why some type of discipline and ordinance had to come about to deal with dissolving marriages.

2) Second, marriage is based on trust and faithfulness. Cultures vary in how they form marriages. In some, the partners marry for love. That's how it is done in our country. But in many countries, that is not the case. Some marriages are arranged. Some marriages are out of what we call a system of castes. If you do fall in love, you can only fall in love within the caste. We find many problems happen when dealing with that kind of thing. However the marriage comes about, once established, God considers it a sacred bond. As a matter of fact, some marriages of this system last much longer than in ours, and we are a God-believing nation. Where marriages are arranged, they last much longer. Sometimes it is the institution that says once you get married, you are to stay married. In some places when the marriage does not work, you die. There is no room to disregard the culture. No room to dissolve that marriage. To dissolve the marriage, you dissolve the culture. In these cultures, if

a man cheats on his wife, he stands before the firing squad. If the woman does the same, she stands before the firing squad. You have disregarded the culture. Yet here we are, a God-believing nation, and marriage is going everywhere. God considers marriage as a bond and expects the partners to honor that union with exclusive, lasting commitment. Marriage is based on trust and faithfulness. Sometimes a marriage may be about to dissolve and it doesn't quite get dissolved. There are so many things amuck. It's hard to build back the trust.

There was a time when a man could get by with certain things, but not these days. The woman is not in the same place economically. Sometimes she would stay in a marriage because it was good for the well-being of the family. Now, however, many women have good jobs and if the husband messes up, she says: "Goodbye, Dude." It has changed. It used to be that the man could divorce his wife and go to another woman because he was still head of the household. I'm just telling you how things have gotten twisted. This is how polygamist marriages have come about. It is against the law in many places. Ultimately, marriage itself is to be built upon trust and faithfulness.

3) Third, we must admit, and we don't like to use the word hate, that God hates unfaithfulness. Just as people marry for various reasons, they divorce for various reasons. The primary reason for divorce, however, is unfaithfulness. Somewhere along the line, unfaithfulness has been proven in the relationship. Not only sexual infidelity but emotional unfaithfulness. God did not put them together to harm each other. God did put them together, and if they keep on hurting each other, they don't know how extensive the pain will become and what they may do. God expects faithfulness and we should, too.

We need to make sure we are teaching and counseling with what the Bible says on the matter of marriage and dissolving a marriage. First, marriage is a holy institution. Next, marriage is built on trust and faithfulness. Finally, God abhors unfaithfulness. If we teach that God is the glue that will make the marriage stick, we will be helping people to focus on God and save their marriages. In premarital counseling, we can make sure to help the couple see this biblical theology on marriage so they can see that it is serious business to God.

ABORTION

Abortion falls into three categories:

1. Voluntary abortion involves the removal of the embryo from the uterus in order to end the pregnancy. "I just want to abort. I don't want to be pregnant. I know they have condoms. I know they have the pill and all that other stuff, but I'm pregnant and I don't want the baby. I have decided I will abort." That is voluntary abortion.

2. Spontaneous abortion deals with a non-viable fetus which leads to miscarriage. "I'm pregnant and I found out that the fetus cannot grow" So after a while, it is considered to be a non-viable fetus. That is called spontaneous abortion.

3. There are some pregnancies in which the fetus is malformed. It looks like it's going to be a monstrous person or thing. It appears that it has no chance of normality in life and so they say, "I will abort this thing." No longer is it called a baby. It is usually called an undesirable thing.

The first area I would like to deal with is voluntary abortion. In my tenure of pastoring, I have had several occasions when people would come to me troubled about their pregnancy. Couples come and say, "We just don't want any babies. We're not ready for babies." We need to stand firm in what the Bible says in this situation. We cannot worry about whether the person will leave our church because of our answer. Remember that if we do not tell them the truth, we will be dealing with a psychological issue. We need to tell the truth of God's Word.

We need to look at the matter of when life begins. I called four doctors to find out what they say about when life begins. Of the four doctors, all but one said it is when the sperm meets the egg that their subject is a living human. Whether it's viable or not comes later. This is why we have various groups - pro-life, pro-choice - all dealing with

> # We cannot worry about whether the person will leave our church because of our answer.

voluntary abortion and when life begins. Even though we hear all these concepts, how will we church leaders treat it? What are church ethics on the matter? All things are lawful, but are not expedient. As a matter of fact, because certain things look like they should be allowed, it doesn't mean that you do it. Many times, we pastors and spokesmen for God have to say, "No. You might feel like it's all right, but it's not right." That is where the rubber meets the road. In dealing with abortion, we need to understand that there is life in the blood, according to the Bible. Once that fetus feeds upon the bloodstream of the female who's carrying it, then blood is involved. Life begins to take its form. Also, the beating of the heart shows that life has formed inside of this body. Exodus 20:13 says, "You shall not murder (NKJ)." If the person's reason to abort is because they just do not want a baby, we are to make it clear that the Bible is against such things. It is murder.

Life is life and not to be taken away.

Does God see it any differently in the case of rape? No. Life is life and not to be taken away, but God did provide a place for a person to go in these cases. Cities of refuge were a safe place for someone to go and live out their pregnancy (Numbers 35). What happens with rape is that a crime has been committed and there are two victims: the woman and the baby. In Old Testament times, the woman could choose to go to the city of refuge and have the baby. She may not have wanted to keep the baby in which case, she would have been put in the care of someone else. In the case of rape, we have to be careful that we do not get so wrapped up in the girl that we forget the baby. We cannot give in and say that it is okay for the girl to abort the baby.

I want to share an experience I had concerning spontaneous abortion. A woman in our church wanted so badly to have a baby. She tried four times and each time she did become pregnant, but then she miscarried. She came to me very upset and I had to tell her, "You are doing more damage to yourself. If it is meant for you to have a baby, and you continue to do this, it's going to be left to you." I have read where after the fourth or fifth try, the baby finally comes. It is not up to our understanding why these things happen. It is the grace of God when a woman has a baby. It is also God's grace when someone does not have a baby. We do not know why the miscarriages took place. Doctors have told women that they were jeopardizing themselves medically for having a baby. It is all up to God and His grace. We need to make sure that we counsel a woman that it is all about the grace of God and if they are meant to have a baby, God will cause it to happen.

Last is the area of deformed fetuses. Aborting a six month old fetus compared to a four week fetus is too difficult. Sometimes, however, the doctor sees a fetus who is malformed, a grotesque-type fetus in the body. Inside the mother, they see a baby formed with four legs, two heads, and those types of things. What does the family decide to do? They might say that the child doesn't have a chance. They decide to abort. Or another decides to have the baby and the baby is born with two heads. As a matter of fact, I just saw a picture where the baby had four arms. How will that child face life? Yet because of religious reasons or whatever, the mother decided to have that baby. Again, life is life. We do not know the reasons for these things, but we do know that all life is given by God.

We see all of these different types of things happening when it comes to one word—abortion. What is your ethical answer as a leader? The main thing is preservation of life. As a parent, you are to give that child the best chance of life. It's going to be left to parents to make a decision that they will live with the rest of their lives. They need to pray that God is pleased with their decision. The pro-choice groups say, "Let me choose whether I want to kill it or not. It's my body." Well, it is not a person's right to have that choice to kill. Just because the condom burst or the pill didn't work and you got pregnant, you do not have the right to end that pregnancy, woman or man. We hear about men putting pressure on their spouse, "I don't want you having a baby because I don't want to take care of one." Let's face it. These are issues that we as leaders are going to have to face. We will give an answer to our decisions. The Bible's response does not change. It's very important that we remember that and answer biblically.

Abortion is a real social and spiritual issue in our society. As pastors and leaders, we need to stand firm on what the Bible says about life. We cannot be like the politicians who have become mute on the subject because they want the votes.

There are many sensitive issues the church leadership must face today. One thing to remember when dealing with any sensitive issue is to keep our eyes on God and what He says about the issues. Our focus must be Christ.

TWO EXTREMES ABOUT SENSITIVE ISSUES

We included this chapter in the book because we believe these sensitive issues must be addressed rather than avoided. People hear of them in the news. They talk about them among themselves. As you lead others in receiving God's truth about such controversial topics, be sure to stay away from two extremes.

1. Some choose obsession

Don't talk about these topics all the time. Too much repetition can cause leaders to be speaking into audiences that no longer hear them. Leaders and preachers who find ways to include one topic or one sin into every sermon or speech should ask themselves why. There are right times and wrong times. There are the right settings and the wrong settings. Sensitive issues should be dealt with – but not too frequently.

2. Some choose avoidance

Don't be afraid to talk about it the right way and at the right time. Notice the examples given in this chapter. Think about the stories you could write. How have you spoken and taught on these subjects correctly? Have you ever spoke about them incorrectly? Have you ever avoided those sensitive topics too often? The right way and the right time and with the right motive: remember those keys. Leaders don't avoid declaring truth. They just want to be sure it is done correctly.

QUESTIONS TO CONSIDER

- What does it mean that "biblical theology is our mainstay?"

- Is your natural tendency to avoid sensitive issues or to address them? What are ways you can improve in that area?

- What are examples from the life of Christ on training young leaders about dealing with sensitive issues?

"*True leadership is tested and proved in crises. The real leader is the one who can handle the stress. He is the one who can solve the problems, bear the burdens, find the solutions, and win the victories when everyone else is merely flustered, confounded, and perplexed.*"

— JOHN MACARTHUR —

CHAPTER SEVEN

A Word About Leaving the Church

We have seen many leaders and pastors leave the church. Who told you that the road would be easy? We have to ask the Lord to help us get out of the way because sometimes things will come up that are too hard for us to take. Many men and women in ministry are willing, but often they put their caps and jackets on and say, "I'm leaving the ministry." They feel the burden is too hard, so they leave, but sometimes after leaving the ministry, they find out that's not the way they should have taken. We have to ask the Lord to help us. We see it, but sometimes we miss the mark by not helping one another enough. There's a heavy mandate to help each other.

In studying and learning history from biblical times, we find that some of the places God guided the apostles are hard to find. Somewhere, but where? We can find out very little about the place, but they became the bishop of that area. It's a fact. It's in the Bible account. I don't see where other apostles poked fun at them. They recognized it was a God-given assignment. We must keep this in mind as we help our brothers and sisters in ministry. Some leaders have been pastoring maybe five or six years and still have only ten members. We want to say it wasn't a God-given thing. We have to be careful about that. That's our personal assumption. That might not be a God-given assignment. God doesn't produce duds. God put in His chosen's mouth to heal flesh and sin. He put in the mouth of His people a heart to bring repentance. Repentance is the heart of the church. For a person to repent, they need to say, "I want to change" and say it so much that they make the effort to change. That's where the leaders come in – God's chosen leaders.

Apostle James was approaching his world with things that were hard to take, but he was a God-given person. God made him a leader. James would let people know that they talked too much and their tongues were getting folks into trouble. As a matter of fact, he said that if you talk out of both sides of your mouth, you are a double-minded person (James 3:1-12). James was quite caustic in his delivery, but he was a God-given leader. We have to understand that God gives the call to be a leader. We should not look at different leaders as God-given because everyone does not have the call.

If it is not their time to finish, they will never be satisfied.

Some may decide to leave the church because they become

discouraged. If the reason is because of what they have gone through personally, then that might not be a good reason to leave. That's a trial of their faith. I've seen people who let pressure make them quit and they're through! If it is not their time to finish, they will never be satisfied. Once you let the work go, you sometimes can't get it back. Sometimes there is someone who wants the leader to let go of the ministry because they want it for themselves. They cannot let that deter them. (Revelations 3:11 NIV). You have to be led and persuaded on your own. Any great leader of God will find out you can never quit. You might step into another role, but you can't quit.

I'm like an old racehorse. I may not be able to run the Kentucky Derby. I may not be able to run the Preakness or the Belmont, but I can still parent. Even though we are not running in those races, we still can produce thoroughbreds. That is why I am sent to leaders of God. God will always put leaders in a position to reproduce.

If you do decide to leave, it will be hard to come back because of your mental state. Once you let go mentally, you might have a difficult time adjusting to return. Also, someone else has your slot. There's a lot involved in it.

I have many friends who have left and tried to come back. They would tell me, "I wish I had done it a little bit differently." We may have to go in where they let go and try to get the congregants to understand that the leader is still there. That is one reason why I am in the position I am in now. I believe the Lord has placed me in a position to help because there are many, many congregations where the pastors have people in place to take over when they leave, but that might not be what God wants. When Moses left, God wanted Joshua to go, even though Caleb was a good man. It takes someone whom God has placed in position to help make sure that church can stay healthy.

If you feel it is time to give up, but you are still energized, do not give up. Just be a parent. It's only good to give up if we are letting God give direction on how to go. We should seek someone who can take our place – someone God wishes to take our place. This is what will keep us healthy and keep our churches healthy in a time of transition.

> It takes someone whom God has placed in position to help make sure that church can stay healthy.

Some leaders leave and give up. I want them to come back even though it isn't always very easy to return. Once you've left, things seem different. Many times you don't want to face the challenges again – some ministers would come back if those challenges would diminish, but the challenges are there for leaders. Don't avoid them. God is with you. See it this way: challenges can help us. To grow can be painful. Keep these two words in mind: growing pains. Those are for leaders. Learn to endure them. Stick with them. It is sad when so many people just can't endure pain. They waver instead of enduring. As true leaders, we can endure.

Those tests we face are difficult. We have a lack of understanding because we try to create an idea that isn't really a part of God's overall plan. We do not want our good to be taken badly. God wants us to be faithful as I learned in the military. He's a loving God, but we need to trust where He is guiding us. What might seem tough in that moment can be protecting us from more pain later. Leaders begin to notice that stuff.

I have served now in the ministry for 42 years. It can be a lonely experience. But you can know that you are not alone. This might feel like a helpless endeavor even though you know that you have help. You know it, but you don't always see them helping or feel the help. For some of us leaders and pastors the loneliness can be overwhelming. If a leader feels that way, I want you to give yourself the luxury of knowing Christ is with you. He will never leave or forsake you – that is the promise given to every leader. No matter how alone you feel, you're walking. That is a welcome sign from God; let Him be with you. We should receive the challenge of letting God be with us instead of letting all those other challenges control us. Leaders often let it overwhelm them. Keep this truth about God being with you no matter how bad it seems to be at this moment. There is joy on the right track. Stay on that right track. Don't get off it.

LEADERS WHO LEAVE

We all know many stories of leaders who have left their positions. Some left because of sin. Some left because of fear. Some left because their selfish motives were not accomplished. Consider these questions when thinking of reasons leaders have left.

1. Were they not trained for the journey?
Go back to their beginning. Many of the points made through this book might have been missed in the early seasons of these leaders' training. If so, they might have entered unprepared. I see that too often. I then go back and pick them up from their years of pain. They can still be retrained and better prepared for future leadership roles.

2. Were they left alone in the battle?
God has called us to live as a community. Many leaders lead alone. Over time, they just can't fight the painful battle

any more. They weren't coached or mentored. No one was there to ask them the difficult questions. They were sent to war all alone. This should not happen, but it is common these days. Be a leader who works to change that.

3. Were they just needing a rest?

Leaders rarely emphasize the importance of Sabbath rest. They are pushed hard and then they are expected to push others hard. They want to succeed and they keep looking for more proof of their success. Do they rest? Do they receive counsel and encouragement from others? If no, they often fall deep into a season of pain. Seek to avoid that. Leaders lead toward rest and peace, not just numbers and goals.

4. Were they just needing a friend?

Again, isolation can lead to a fall. True friends can lead others by lovingly mentoring them. Teams are crucial. But all the talk should not be about the ministry or business goals. Outcome isn't all there is to life. Friends can help other leaders before their load gets too heavy. Train young leaders early on the importance of needing a friend with whom they can talk.

QUESTIONS TO CONSIDER

- What does this statement mean to you? "God gives the call to be a leader."

- Think about a story in your life when a leader left for poor reasons. How did their departure make you feel? What do you wish had been done differently? What can you learn from their situation?

- Write a list of practical ways you believe God can help you endure and not give up.

CONTINUE THE CONVERSATION

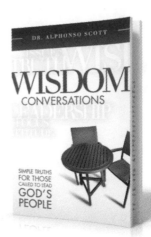

If you believe in the message of this book and would like to share in the ministry of getting this important message out, please consider taking part by:

- Writing about *Wisdom Conversations* on your blog, Twitter, and Facebook page.

- Suggesting *Wisdom Conversations* to friends and send them to the book's website **livelystone.org.**

- When you're in a bookstore, ask them if they carry the book. The book is available through all major distributors, so any bookstore that does not have it in stock can easily order it.

- Writing a positive review on www.amazon.com.

- Purchasing additional copies to give away as gifts.